THE HARDEST PART

G. A. Studdert Kennedy

Copyright © 2015 Beloved Publishing

All rights reserved. No part of this book may be reproduced, scanned, or distributed in any printed or electronic form without permission.

Printed in the United States of America

ISBN: 9781631741050

The sorrows of God mun be 'ard to bear
If 'e really 'as love 'is 'eart
And the 'ardest part in the world to play
Mun surely be God's Part.

TO MY WIFE

Contents:

Preface . . . 1
Author's Introduction . . . 3

I: What is God Like? . . . 7
II: God in Nature . . . 15
III: God in History . . . 23
IV: God in the Bible . . . 33
V: God and Democracy . . . 45
VI: God and Prayer . . . 59
VII: God and the Sacrament . . . 69
VIII: God and the Church . . . 81
IX: God and the Life Eternal . . . 91

Postscript . . . 105

Preface

THIS collection of essays needs no preface, but as Studdert Kennedy has asked me to write one, I can perhaps best comply with his request by telling those who read this book something about the man who wrote it.

Of Irish extraction he was brought up in Leeds, where his father was vicar of a parish in a poor district. Kennedy was educated at Leeds Grammar School and Trinity College, Dublin. In 1908 he was ordained by the Bishop of Worcester and went to work at Rugby under the present Dean of Windsor.

He eventually returned to assist his father in his slum parish in Leeds, and in 1914 he was appointed Vicar of St. Paul s, Worcester, a very poor parish of some 3,000 souls.

As a parish priest Studdert Kennedy proved himself a diligent visitor, who by his sympathy and unselfish devotion won the hearts of many. He is a speaker of extraordinary power, and I know none so effective with men. His powers of vivid description, his absolute naturalness and manifest sincerity attract and interest.

In the early days of the war, when a large number of men were in training at Worcester, some 2,000 attended the Cathedral on Sunday mornings. When Kennedy preached, as he sometimes did, Church Parade lost all its stiffness and boredom, every man was all attention, and the addresses with their racy remarks and telling illustrations were the chief topic of conversation during the ensuing week.

At the end of 1915 Kennedy, having been able to make arrangements for the duties of his parish, went out as a chaplain. His geniality and good fellow ship endeared him to the men, and his bravery and sincerity won their respect. He went through a good deal of fight ing, and the brutal realities of war brought him face to face with the problem of reconciling belief in the love of God with the omnipotence of the Deity.

These essays are an attempt by a thoroughly religious man to solve this and other problems, and bring religion into relation to the stern realities of life, and free it from deadening conventionalities in thought and practice. These pages express the thoughts which came to the writer amid the hardships of the trenches and the brutalities of war. It is literally theology hammered out on the field of battle.

Some may disapprove of what he has written and dissent from his conclusions, but they will profit by reading the book and learning how an earnest man endeavours to do for the British soldier what the writer of the book of Job and the prophet Isaiah endeavoured to do for the men of their times.

Kennedy expresses in a striking and graphic manner what multitudes who have not his power of expression are dumbly thinking.

Expert theologians before condemning should read the author's postscript. Its revelation of the spirit of the man and his object in writing will do much to disarm criticism.

W. MOORE EDE.

DEANEBY, WORCESTER.
May 1918.

Author's Introduction

WHEN I had been in France as a chaplain about two months, before I had heard a gun fired or seen a trench, I went to see an officer in a base hospital who was slowly recovering from very serious wounds. The conversation turned on religion, and he seemed anxious to get at the truth. He asked me a tremendous question. " What I want to know, Padre," he said, " is, what is God like ? I never thought much about it before this war. I took the world for granted. I was not religious, though I was confirmed and went to Communion some times with my wife. But now it all seems different. I realise that I am a member of the human race, and have a duty towards it, and that makes me want to know what God is like. When I am transferred into a new battalion I want to know what the Colonel is like. He bosses the show, and it makes a lot of difference to me what sort he is. Now I realise that I am in the battalion of humanity, and I want to know what the Colonel of the world is like. That is your real business, Padre ; you ought to know."

I think that this question sums up in a wonderful way the form which the spiritual revival is taking among men at the front. First there comes a wider vision of humanity. This arises partly from the new sense of comradeship and brotherhood which exists in our new citizen armies, and unites them with the citizen armies of the allied nations, and partly from the world-wide scale of this tremendous conflict. The cutting of the world in two by the sword has helped men to see it whole. Mens minds are of necessity less parochial, less insular, and more cosmopolitan, in the best sense, than they were. As a consequence of this there is a quickened interest in ultimate questions, a desire to know the meaning of it all. This grows in some cases to a positive hunger for the knowledge of God and a conscious seeking after Him; in others it remains a kind of dim dumb longing for some ultimate truth. Finally, there is a certain, partly wistful, partly disappointed, turning to the Churches in the rather forlorn hope of obtaining information and light. Sometimes the question is put to the Church anxiously and sadly, sometimes with bitterness and contempt.

In the vast majority of cases, of course, it is not put in words, because those who would ask it have no words in which to express it. It appears rather in the attitude of mind, and is hinted at in the conversation of these splendidly dumb soldiers who act and cannot speak. But the question is there in the heart of the army and of the nation, " What is God like? "

When a chaplain joins a battalion no one says a word to him about God, but every one asks him, in a thousand different ways, " What is God like ? " His success or failure as a chaplain really depends upon the answer He gives by word and by deed. The answer by deed is the more important, but an answer by words is inevitable, and must be given somehow.

When the question was put to me in hospital I pointed to a crucifix which hung over the officer s bed, and said, " Yes, I think I can tell you. God is like that." I wondered if it would satisfy him. It did not. He was silent for a while, looking at the crucifix, and then he turned to me, and his face was full of doubt and disappointment. " What do you mean ? " he said ; " God cannot be like that. God is Almighty, Maker of heaven and earth, Monarch of the world, the King of kings, the Lord of lords, Whose will sways all the world. That is a battered, wounded, bleeding figure, nailed to a cross and helpless, defeated by the world and broken in all but spirit. That is not God ; it is part of God's plan : God's mysterious, repulsive, and apparently perfectly futile plan for saving the world from sin. I cannot understand the plan, and it appears to be a thoroughly bad one, because it has not saved the world from sin. It has been an accomplished fact now for nearly two thousand years, and we have sung hymns about God s victory, and yet the world is full of sin, and now there is this filthy war. I m sick of this cant. You have not been up there, Padre, and you know nothing about it. I tell you that cross does not help me a bit ; it makes things worse. I admire Jesus of Nazareth ; I think He was splendid, as my friends at the front are splendid splendid in their courage, patience, and unbroken spirit. But I asked you not what Jesus was like, but what God is like, God Who willed His death in agony upon the Cross, and Who apparently wills the wholesale slaughter in this war. Jesus Christ I know and admire, but what is God Almighty like ? To me He is still the un known God."

How would you answer him ? How would you answer the thousands like him, who feel all that but cannot put their feelings into words ? That is what I have tried to do in this small book. For two years I have been serving with the army, always learning more than I could teach. Part of the time I have been with the men in the line, part of it I served at the base, and part I spent touring about from base to front and from front to base, preaching to great crowds of men, and trying to answer their questions. I have learned a great deal about the mind of the ordinary man, and I have learned to love and respect him, and to be ashamed of my
self.

All my experience has grouped itself round and hinged itself upon the answer to this question, asked me at the beginning, " What is God like ? " because it appears to me to be the only question that ultimately and really matters and must be answered. The form of meditations in battle which the answer takes is the result of an experience which much surprised me. During active operations I was very busy and intensely preoccupied, and unconscious of any connected thinking, and yet when a lull came I found in my memory whole trains of thought that had been working themselves out all the time. Each train of thought I have tried to write down as memory gave it to me, without elaboration, and they fall into a kind of reasonable sequence.

I only hope that what I have written may help those who are dumbly asking this great question, and those who are trying to answer it for them. It is all of necessity very sketchy and incomplete, but I hope and pray it may serve to help those in difficulty, as the vision of God I have tried to express has helped me.

G. A. STUDDERT KENNEDY, C.F.,

Army Infantry School, B.E.F.

I: What is God Like?

June 7th, 1917.

IN the assembly trenches on the morning of the attack on the Whyschaete-Messines Ridge. The division attacked first, and our men went through their lines to the last objective.

It is God alone that matters. I am quite sure about that. I m not sure that it is not the only thing I am sure about. It is not any Church of God, or priest of God ; it is not even any act of God in the past like the Birth of Christ or His death upon the Cross. These may be revelations of what God is or means by which He works ; but it is God Himself, acting here and now upon the souls of men ; it is He alone that can save the world.

There is only one commandment really : Thou shalt love the Lord thy God with all thy heart, with all thy mind, with all thy
strength with the whole bag of tricks in fact. It s got to be a whole hog, go-ahead and damn the consequences kind of love a complete and enthusiastic surrender of the whole man to the leadership of God. It is funny the body isn t mentioned ; it comes in here a bit, the giving of the body. It s about all some of these dear chaps know how to give, and they give like kings : better than many kings, God bless em. There is the whole of vital religion, and therefore the whole of life, in a nutshell Love God all out, and then live with all your might. The other commandment is only a bit off the big one. You couldn't help loving your neighbour if you once loved God. You may love churches and services and hymns and things, and not love your neighbour ; lots of people do, but that is not loving God. These things be come ends in themselves,

The Hardest Part

and then they are worse than useless. That s always been the bother with religion.

It s a difficult business. I suppose loving God means knowing God. You can't love a person unless you know him. How can
a man know God ? "By their fruits ye shall know them." I suppose that rule applies. By God s fruits ye shall know Him. That is the queerest yet. It fairly beats the band God s fruits. Where do they begin, and where do they end ?

———————

I suppose it must be getting on time now. Five minutes past three, I make it, and ten minutes past is zero. It will be the devil of a shindy when it starts. What a glorious morning ! So still. Now the birds are just awaking in English Wood. How soft the silver dawn light is, and this grey mist that hangs so low makes all the open meadow land just like a dim- lit sea, with clumps of trees for islands. In the east there is a flush of red blood red. Blood . . . Beauty . . . God s Fruits. I wonder what

———————

God Almighty ! what s that ? It s the Hill gone up. Lord, what a noise! and all the earth is shaking. It must be like that Korah, Dathan, and Abiram business in the Book of Numbers up there. All the lot went down, women and children and all. I always thought it was hard luck on the children. It s like war though. War is just a mighty earthquake that swallows all before it. Now for it. Here come the guns. Listen to that big 12-inch. It sounds like the man with a loud voice and no brains in an argument. I thought I'd get the wind up, and here I am laughing. We re all laughing. We re en joying it. That s the stuff to give em. It is a glorious sight, one silver sheet of leaping flame against the blackness of the trees. But it

s damnable, it s a disgrace to civilisation. It's murder wholesale murder. We can t see the other end ugh damn all war! They have wives and kiddies like my Patrick, and they are being torn to bits and tortured. It s damnable. What's that, lad ? Shout a bit louder. It is, you re right, it is the stuff to give em.
They can t stand much of that; they'll have to quit.

How wonderful that sky is, golden red, and all the grass is diamond-spangled like the gorgeous robe that clothes a king. Solomon in all his glory. Look at that lark. Up he goes. He doesn't care a tuppeny dump for the guns. His song is drowned, but not his joy.

> God s in His heaven ;
> All s right with the

What awful nonsense ! All s right with the world, and this ghastly, hideous But, by George, it s a glorious barrage, and English girls made em. We re all in it sweethearts, mothers, and wives. The hand that rocks the cradle wrecks the world. There are no non-combatants. We re all in it, and God, God Almighty, the loving Father Who takes count of every sparrows fall, what is He doing ? It is hard to fathom. God s fruits, singing birds and splendid beauty, flowers and fair summer skies, golden mists and bloody slaughter ! What is a man to make of it ?

"Almighty and everlasting God, we are taught by Thy holy word that the hearts of kings and governors are in Thy rule and governance, and that Thou dost dispose and turn them as

The Hardest Part

it seemeth best to Thy godly wisdom." ... I think that s right. It s in the Communion Service, anyhow. I suppose it includes the Kaiser. Anyhow, it is nonsense. What unspeakable blackguards some kingsand governors have been, and what utter ruin they have caused ! Why should we start a prayer with such a futile falsehood ? Their hearts can t be in God s rule and governance when they are evil and base. There it is in the Communion Service. If it is true, what is God like ?

What is God like? I remember that's what that officer in hospital asked me." You ought to know ; that is your business, Padre," he said. I suppose it is, and I ought to know. But do I ? Do I know and love God ? Jesus Christ I know and love. He is splendid. I love His superb courage, His majestic patience, and His perfect love. I love His terrible wrath against all wrong and His tender kindness to the weak. Tender as a woman and terrible as a thunderstorm, Jesus Christ, I know and love ; but Almighty and Everlasting God, High and Mighty, King of kings and Lord of lords, the only Ruler of princes, to Whom all things in heaven and earth and under the earth do bow and obey, do I know anything at all about Him ? Do I believe in Him ? How can I find Him in this welter of sin and cruelty. I have said such words a thousand times. What did I mean ? What did the men who wrote them mean ? It all seems like silly sentimental nonsense in the face of this.

They are supposed to be expressions of reverence. Just now they sound like expressions of blasphemy, accusations against God. Are they superficial compliments necessary in the court of the Most High ? How God must hate them if they aren t true ! and how can they be true ? I wish they would not put such things in the Prayer Book. It makes one sick in the light of scenes like this. This war is the very devil ; it seems to scupper all one s ancient understandings.

The Hardest Part

We're off now, over the top. I think I'm frightened. But that s bosh. I can t die. That s another thing I m sure about." Thanks be to God Who giveth us the victory through Our Lord Jesus Christ." Any how, I m a skunk to think about that now. What does it matter if I do die ? . . . except to her . . . and it is better for her and the boy for me to go out decent and respectable than to have me live on a beastly funk ; so come on, you silly old fool, come on. Lord, that boy looks bad. Buck up, lad, it will be all right. We've got em stiff. Look at that chap s boots, all bust at the back, and his feet are blistered too, I bet, and that pack, and ammunition, like a traveling cheap jack. What torture ! I say, damn all war, and those that make it ! The kings and governors whose hearts God is supposed to turn and govern. Come on, you chaps. That barrage is perfect. A cat couldn't live in it. Now we're well away. Lord, what a howling wilderness the guns have made !

    It's about my time to strike off to the left on my own. There s the wood in which I've got to find a place for an Aid Post. It's being shelled pretty heavily. I believe I m getting windy again. Damn all nerves ! Dear Christ, Who suffered on the Cross and wouldn't take that sleeping stuff, give me strength to be a decent chap. Come on. How I hate being alone. It's rotten. One pal makes all the difference. But He was alone. It s funny how it is always Christ upon the Cross that comforts ; never God upon a throne. One needs a Father, and a Father must suffer in His children s suffering. I could not worship the passionless potentate.

He who did most has borne most, the strongest has stood the most weak ;
"Tis that weakness in strength that I cry for, my flesh that I seek.

In the Godhead—I seek it and find it.

I don t know or love the Almighty potentate my only real God is the suffering Father revealed in the sorrow of Christ. That was a near one. These Boche shells can t have as much in them as they used to have or I would be " To-day thou shalt be with Me in Paradise." Yes, that s it.

Good Lord, what's that ? A dead Boche. I kicked him hard, poor little devil. He lies like a tired child that has cried itself to sleep. He looks puzzled, as if he were asking, Why me ? My God, my God, why me ? What had he to do with it, anyhow ? Not much great blond beast about him, He couldn't hurt a decent well-developed baby. That little chap is the very fly blown incarnation of the filth of war. You can see all Europe asking questions in his weak blue eyes. War serves them all alike ; good and bad, guilty and innocent, they all go down together in this muddy, bloody welter of mad misery. How can a man believe in an absolute Almighty God ? What is He doing? " Perad venture He sleepeth." The God that answers by fire let Him be God. It is an odd thing God doesn t seem to work that way now. It would be a simple way of solving things, but Heaven makes no sign.

Here s the very place I m looking for. It will make a splendid Aid Post. I wish it was not shelled so heavily. The Red Cross makes no odds. Nothing makes much odds. God Himself seems non-existent the Al mighty Ruler Whom all things obey. He seems to have gone to sleep and allowed all things to run amuck. I don t believe there is an absolute Almighty Ruler. I don't see how any one can believe it. If it were a choice between that God and no God, I would be an atheist.

But how near the God Whom Christ revealed comes at a time like this : nearer than breathing, nearer than hands and feet, the Father of sorrow and love Who spoke through the crucified Son.

O Christ my God, my only God, so near, so suffering, and so strong, come down into my soul, and into the souls of all my comrades, and make us strong to suffer for honour and for right. Christ the Lord of courage, kill my fear and make me now and always indifferent to death that I may live and die like Thee.

That is the lot now, Doc. The sergeant died, so we did not bring him down. I ll bury him up there to-morrow. It s quiet now. They re all going well over. What a lovely night ! A million stars, like an army with torches marching through the darkness to the dawn. Points of light they seem, and they are shining worlds. All our astronomy does not bring us much nearer to the truth. I suppose all astronomy started with

> Twinkle, twinkle, little star,
> How I wonder what you are.

And it leaves us wondering still only more so. Almighty God ! When you look at them, " Almighty " seems the right word still. It kind of says the mystery right, the mystery of life that science only makes more deep. God s fruits, the silent silver beauty of the stars, but ugh ! how that poor chap groans. All my togs are covered with his blood. Doc, I m going to sleep. Call me in an hour. "Father, into Thy hands." It's always the Cross in the end God, not Almighty, but God the Father, with a Father's sorrow and a Fathers weakness, which is the strength of love ; God splendid, suffering, crucified Christ. . . There's the Dawn.

The Hardest Part

II: God in Nature

June 15th, 1917.

IN a shell hole near the pill-box which was B.H.Q. The dawn of day after a battle. All night the evacuation of the wounded had gone on without a stop. There were many casualties.

I don't believe I could carry another one to save my life. Lord, how my shoulders ache. I wish I were Sandow. It s a good thing there are no more to carry. I wonder will that last chap live ? His thigh seemed all mash when we pulled him in. It was a beastly job. He cried for mercy and we had to drag on just the same. He is strong though, a splendid body all broken up. It s quiet now, only for those 5 9 s over on the right. They never stop. I m glad to sit and think. How I do love quiet. What a perfect morning it is. All the sky burns red with the after-blush of dawn, and here I seem surrounded by a soft grey sea of mist. What unutterable beauty there is in Nature. No wonder artists despair. God s fruits. I suppose the first of all God s fruits by which we may know Him is the world of Nature. Nature drives a man to belief in something, or rather some one, behind it all.

The basis of religion is Nature worship. H. G. Wells wants me to give up wondering who made the world, because it has nothing to do with religion, being a purely scientific question. What a comic person he is in many ways. He is the most utterly civilised man I know. He is as civilised as Piccadilly. He could never write poetry or really understand religion ; they are both too primitive. Like most apostles of the superman he is not really advanced so much as defective. He wants to build a future which has no real relation to the past. I wish he could have come out here ; it would have given him the knowledge of naked Nature that he lacks. He might have understood religion because he has a soul, only it is a soul that has always lived in streets.

You cannot leave Nature out of religion when you love it, and all natural men do. The natural man's first argument for God
is always flowers or trees or brussels sprouts or something. You have to worship Nature or the Maker of it. It calls you. You are part of it. You draw your very life, your power to worship and adore, from the vitals of this poor battered earth. Nature means well, and the beauty of its million colours and the music of its million sounds just pull your heart-strings and you have to worship. It will take more than Wells to still the pipes of Pan, and they play the oldest religious music in the world. " Behold the lilies of the field ; they toil not, neither do they spin ; yet I say unto you that Solomon in all his glory was not arrayed like one of these." So the pipes of Pan found echo in the soul of Jesus Christ. You can't leave Nature out. It's like telling a man to leave out his heart and
lop along with his liver. Nature is one of God's fruits by which we have to know Him. I know it is hard to see in Nature what God is ; its many voices seem to contradict one another. Its tenderness and cruelty, its order and its chaos, its beauty and its ugliness, make discords in its song and mar the music of its message to the soul of man. There is much truth in the charge that Nature is red in tooth and claw. It is hard to see God in a cobra or a shark.

Nevertheless, the heart of the ordinary man will always turn away from these things and come back to the glory of a summer dawn and worship the Maker of it. " The Veiled Being," Wells calls Him, and He may be that ; but still I stretch my hands out toward the veil and worship Him in gratitude, although I cannot see His face. I've got to worship Him. It isn't my intellect that wants Him, it's my " me," my innermost essential me. I want to paint or draw or put into words some expression of my love and praise. It calls and grips. For me the world will always be a vast and star-lit temple where every bush and flower flames with God, and I believe in that I am just an extension of the average man.

Still, there is truth in the statement that Nature's God must always be an unknown God, because the revelation of God in Nature is a contradiction of itself. It looks like that on the surface. Flowers and summer skies tell of a God of beauty and love, but
snakes and earthquakes, volcanoes, plagues, and floods cry out against that message. The lamb and the lion do not lie down together, but are at war. I can remember how Haeckel's *Riddle of the Universe* shook my faith in God. "The cruel and pitiless struggle for existence which rages through all living nature, and which must for ever rage ... is an undeniable fact." I remember that sentence, and it seems so true. It is all war, and it does look heartless and cruel.

But is not the difficulty really in the at tempt to see in Nature an Almighty God a Being Who can do everything which we imagine to be possible, a God Who could have made a perfect, painless, sinless world at a stroke, but Who, for some inexplicable reason, chose to adopt this slow, tortuous, and painful method of evolutionary creation. We are invited to find a meaning and a use for everything in Nature even sharks and poisonous snakes. We are asked to regard floods, famines, pestilence, and disease as visitations of the Almighty, exhibitions of His supreme power. We are told that Nature is a perfect system of balances in which there is a place for everything and everything has its place. There is supposed to be no failure and no possibility of failure in Nature, inasmuch as every detail of it is the work of absolute omnipotence. The result of this attempt to adapt Nature to an imaginary conception of God based upon abstractions is utter be wilderment. The materialism of Haeckel and the pseudo-Darwinites seems honest and illuminating beside it. Men still prefer materialism to this blind piety, because, sad and hopeless as its teaching is, it does at least seem to be honest and to face the fact of Nature's horror chambers unafraid.

The Hardest Part

Yet materialism is hopeless even from a purely intellectual point of view. Mechanical evolution is as incredible as the six days creation. Darwin seemed sufficient for the eyes of a cod-fish, but he won t do for Coleridge s poems or the eyes of Jesus Christ.

And they are all part of one big show. You cannot separate the cod-fish from Coleridge, or snakes from Shakespeare. The attempt to believe that " Macbeth " or "The Hound of Heaven" is the result of a mechanical process gives me intellectual dyspepsia. It is easier to believe the Virgin Birth, and that s hard enough. Science has not really answered a single ultimate question. It leaves us where we were before. It is incurably abstract, and can only work by abstraction ; which means taking out what you don't want and leaving in what you do. Real Nature refuses to be bound down to a rigid system of laws. They suffice for rough results in practice, but they don t come near the truth. Queer things happen in the universe, and science is against what's queer. That is why, from the human stand point, it is often such an insufferable bore. It wears gold spectacles, doesn't believe in fairies, and tries not to look startled when something in Nature jumps, or a man displays superb self-sacrifice and disregards the natural laws which made him. This system of mechanical creation gave Europe an awful fright in the nineteenth century. We thought we would have to worship an engine an engine ! not even an engine-driver. Personally, I might have managed an engine-driver. Engine-drivers are alive, and do strange things. I knew one who used to get drunk and spit in unexpected places. I did not worship him, but I did like him. He was at any rate a person. But worshipping an engine, a mechanical system, makes me feel like a cog a little cog in a big wheel. That is what it does make men feel. It is soul-destroying, because it denies liberty. It is German ; that's what it is ; in fact, it s the devil. It is as intellectually impressive and as vitally futile as Pan-Germanism, because it has no psychology, and does not believe in freedom or in souls.

The Hardest Part

The truth is, that the piety which bade us find in Nature absolutely omnipotent benevolence is maddening, because it will not face the facts of Nature s failures and refuses to look into its horror chambers ; while materialism is even more maddening, because it will not face the facts of Natures most astounding successes nor look into its treasure stores of wonder and beauty with open eyes.

We must look at both. I am sure that Lamarck was nearer than Darwin, and that what is behind the Universe is a will or a wish. It is not an accident or a series of accidents, it is a design. But there is no use pretending that it is a perfectly expressed design. I agree with old Lucretius there ; I cannot believe the world is perfect *tantis stat prcedita culpis* it has too many faults. Behind all the vast history of effort, ceaseless effort, that Science has disclosed, I can see a will, but not an absolutely omnipotent will that knows no failure and no strain. I cannot see the calm, serene, untroubled potentate whose word at once creates perfection. The paths of natural development are strewn with species that have failed, like the dead horses on the road from Hell-fire Corner to the line. The story of this strange world s growth, as I have read it, is the story of a ceaseless war, with perfection of personality as its end in view. It is the story of many failures, out of which has come success ; it is a tale of mysterious obstacles marvellously overcome, and of victory wrung by stupendous effort from the very heart of defeat. Nature is a triumph, a victory over enemies and obstacles the nature of which we cannot comprehend. The Spirit that labours behind Nature seems always to be up against difficulties, the utter necessity of which we cannot grasp because they arise from the nature of matter which is the final mystery the thing we do not understand at all. I believe H. G. Wells is right when he sees in the crucified Christ the revelation of the true God, bearing titanic pain and nailed upon a cross of matter, if only we remember that behind the Cross there is the Empty Tomb, and that Christ, Who suffered pain and death, rose again unconquered, to go on suffering and conquering down the ages.

That is the picture of God which Nature gives when you look square in her face and refuse to blind yourself either to her failure or her success. God was forced to limit Himself when He undertook the task of material creation. He had to bind Him self with chains and pierce Himself with nails, and take upon Himself the travail pangs of creation. The universe was made as it is because it is the only way it could be made, and this way lays upon God the burden of many failures and of eternal strain the sorrow of God the Father which Christ revealed. That is why one s heart goes out in love to the -Spirit that labours behind Nature. If one believed Him to be the absolute omnipotent monarch seated on a throne, high and lifted up in power, and capable of accomplishing absolute perfection at a stroke, then one would curse Him for Nature s manifest imperfections and many cruelties floods, famines, volcanic eruptions, disease, plague, pestilence, and the like. All these horrors which He could prevent, and will not, one would curse Him for, and rightly so.

> But Thou, with strong prayer and very much entreating,
>   Wiliest be asked, and Thou wilt answer then ;
>   Show the hid heart behind creation beating,
>   Smile with kind eyes and be a Man with men.
>
>   Were it not thus, O King of my salvation,
>   Many would curse to Thee; and I, for one,
> Would spit on Thy bliss and snatch at Thy damnation,
>   Scorn and abhor the shining of the sun.

When in Nature one sees God suffering and striving as a creative Father Spirit, and when one sees how much that His sorrow has produced is quite perfect, like this red dawn and that white bird upon the wing, the rose that blooms at the cottage door, and the glory of sweet spring days, and the eyes of my dog, and the neck of my horse, and a million other perfect things and when one sees all this as the fruit not only of God s power, but also of God s pain, then the love of Nature s God begins to grow up in one s soul. One remembers the great words, " He that hath seen Me hath seen the Father," and there comes a burst of light, and one sees Nature in Christ, and Christ in Nature. One sees in Christ the Revelation of suffering, striving, tortured, but triumphant Love which Nature itself would lead us to expect. I can see the face of Jesus Christ staring up at me out of the pages of a scientific text-book which tells me the story of the patient, painful progress of a great plan.

I have no fear of Nature s horror chambers ; they are just God s Cross, and I know that the Cross is followed by an Empty Tomb and victory. God is limited now, and has been ever since creation began, by the necessities inherent in His task ; but those necessities are not eternal, they are only temporary and contingent, and God will overcome them in the end. That is our faith. He that hath seen Christ has seen the Father, and Christ not only died, but conquered death and rose again. God the Father is suffering, striving, crucified, but unconquerable. We see His triumph now in Nature s glory, and we hear Him calling to us to join Him in the task of conquering the evils which arise from the necessities of creation. He calls us to combat floods and famines and pestilence and disease. He hates them, and wills with us to overcome them, and they shall be overcome. The Doctor, the Pioneer,the Scientist, are workers with God like the Priest. All good work is God s work, and all good workers do God's will. They are labouring to make a world. That seems to me to be the truth of God in Nature, the truth of Christ crucified and risen again to reveal the suffering but triumphant Father. In the light of the Cross and the Resurrection Nature s many voices make no discords, they all tone into one, and that is the voice of Christ.

The Hardest Part

What's that, Colonel ? Breakfast ? I'm coming. I m hungry, too. Good old earth, what would I do without you ? Poor old patient mother earth, with all your beauty battered into barrenness by man s insanity. He who made you is not dead, though crucified afresh. Some day He will rise again for you, and all this wilderness that man has made will blossom like the rose, and this valley will laugh with laughter of summer woods and golden grain, and cottage homes in whose bright gardens children play at peace and unafraid. Yes, I'm coming, Colonel. What is it ? Bacon and eggs ? Good old pigs and hens.

III: God in History

IN a German concrete shelter. Time, 2.30 a.m. All night we had been making un successful attempts to bring down some wounded men from the line. We could not get them through the shelling. One was blown to pieces as he lay on his stretcher.

I wonder how much this beastly shanty would stand. I guess it would come in on us with a direct hit, and it looks like getting one soon. Lord, that was near it. Here, somebody light that candle again. I wish we could have got those chaps down. It was murder to attempt it though. That poor lad, all blown to bits I wonder who he was. God, it s awful. The glory of war, what utter blather it all is. That chap in the " Soldiers Three " was about right :

> Says Mooney, I declare,
> The death is everywhere;
> But the glory never seems to be about.

War is only glorious when you buy it in the Daily Mail and enjoy it at the break fast-table. It goes splendidly with bacon and eggs. Real war is the final limit of damnable brutality, and that s all there is in it. It s about the silliest, filthiest, most inhumanly fatuous thing that ever happened. It makes the whole universe seem like a mad muddle. One feels that all talk of order and meaning in life is insane sentimentality.

It's not as if this were the only war. It s not as if war were extraordinary or abnormal. It's as ordinary and as normal as man. In the days of peace before this war we had come to think of it as abnormal and extraordinary. We had read The Great Illusion, and were all agreed that war was an anachronism in a civilised world. We had got past it. It was primitive, and would not, could not, come again on a large scale. It is " The Great Illusion " right enough, and it is an anachronism in a civilised world. We ought to have got past it ; but we haven t. It has come again on a gigantic scale.

I say, keep that door shut; the light can be seen. I believe they are right on to this place. There was a German sausage up all day just opposite, and they must have spotted movement hereabouts this morning. There it goes again. Snakes, that s my foot you re standing on. Any body hurt ? Right-o, light the candle. It s no fun smoking in the dark.

Yes, war has come again all right. It's the rule with man, not the exception. The history of man is the history of war as far
back as we can trace it. Christ made no difference to that. There never has been peace on earth. Christ could not conquer war. He gave us chivalry, and produced the sporting soldier ; but even that seems dead. Chivalry and poison gas don't go well together. Christ Himself was turned into a warrior and led men out to war. Few wars have been so fierce and so prolonged as the so-called religious wars. Of course a deeper study of history reveals the fact that they were not really religious wars. Religion was not the real, but only the apparent cause of them. They were just political and commercial struggles waged under the cloak of religion. I don't believe that religion had anything to do with the Inquisition, it was a political business throughout. Still these struggles, with all their sordid brutalities, proved Christ helpless against the God of War. He is helpless still. God is helpless to prevent war, or else He wills it and approves of it. There is the alternative. You pay your money and you take your choice.

Christians in the past have taken the second alternative, and have stoutly declared that God wills war. They have quoted Christ as saying that He came not to bring peace upon the earth, but a sword. Bernhardi did that quite lately. Luther did it too, I believe. If you cling to God s absolute omnipotence, you must do it. If God is absolutely omnipotent, He must will war, since war is and always has been the commonplace of history. Men are driven to the conclusion that war is the will of the Almighty God.

If it is true, I go morally mad. Good and evil cease to have any meaning. If anything is evil, war is. It is supposed to be a blessing to the nations by those who advocate or apologise for it. It is supposed to make them virile and strong. It is a strange method of doing it, to take all your finest physical and spiritual specimens and set them to kill one another by thousands, and leave weaklings alive to breed the race of the future. It is the best and most direct way of securing the survival of the unfittest. Specially under modern conditions, when by mechanical contrivances weaklings can slaughter splendid men by scores with shells hurled at them from miles away. War is evil. It is a cruel and insane waste of energy and life. If God wills war, then I am morally mad and life has no meaning. I hate war, and if God wills it I hate God, and I am a better man for hating Him ; that is the pass it brings me to. In that case the first and great commandment is, " Thou shalt hate the Lord thy God with all thy heart, and Him only shalt Thou detest and despise."

Then I give it up. I can t see God, and I can't love Him. I turn back to Christ. I can see Him and love Him. He could not will war. He brought strife upon earth, because He roused the powers of evil by, challenging them ; but He did not will strife : He suffered agony and death because of it, and pleaded with men to conquer evil and; learn to live at peace.

This is the only attitude I can accept without degradation, and if that is not God s attitude, if God does not suffer agony because of war, and if He does not will that men should live at peace, then I cannot and will not worship Him. I hate Him. This is not merely an intellectual alternative, it is a moral one. It lives and burns. It is a matter of life and death which side you take. If it were merely intellectual it would not matter.

The Hardest Part

Intellectually the Almighty God Who wills war has a lot to say for Himself. Heinrich von Treitschke is His prophet, and the Prussians are His chosen people. They have a splendid case. The militarist interpretation of history is an inevitable result of the doctrine of the absolute omnipotence of God.

Progress has everywhere and at all times been accompanied by strife and warfare. It is the eternal law of nature. The struggle
for existence and the survival of the fittest are Almighty God s appointed methods of progress. The strong man must survive and the weaker go to the wall. That is the law of nature, and therefore the will of God. How can you argue against that ? You can't. You can only oppose sentiment to reason, and that fight is won before it is fought for any reasonable man. This world is not a Sunday School ; it is a slaughter-house, and always has been. Peace or war, what does it matter ? There is no such thing as peace, and never can be. Competition is just peaceful war with far more cruel weapons than either shot or shell. War is competition stripped of all disguise without the velvet glove. Who is going to deny that competition is the law of business and the law of life ? A few parsons perhaps, and some socialists who want what they have not got. Every sensible man of the world knows that cut-throat competition is the law of life, the cause of progress, and the only real motive of efficiency and work.

You cannot kill knowledge with rhetoric or alter facts by furious abuse. You may rail at the Prussian, but at least he is no
hypocrite. He is the honest man of Europe, or at least he was until he was beaten and began to whine. There was no Sunday- School sentiment about him. He did not pretend to apply the teachings of a visionary Christ to practical politics. He took his stand on the rocks of natural fact, and claimed the support of the Al mighty God according to Whose will the everlasting strife of history has been the lot of man. It is absurd to charge the Kaiser with hypocrisy when he claims

26

that God is with him. If God be absolutely Almighty, then He is with him, and was when he declared war, it being the will of God that the strong should seek to conquer the weak. The Kaiser is right when you look at the thing honestly in the cold light of reason, and refuse to use sentiment and religious soft soap.

The Prussian is the really consistent worshipper of the Almighty God Whom Nature plainly reveals as the Author of life. He believes in power, patiently makes him self powerful, and then puts power to the test. If he loses then, it is because he is not powerful enough, and he must set to work again. In the end power must prevail, for that is God s will in the world. Might is right.

And what about the British ? We are the hypocrites. God is Love, we say. Right is might. But do we trust in right, or in Love ? Not much.

Let us have done with this nonsense. Let us have a bit of Prussian honesty. They are the sincere and consistent worshippers of the Almighty God of strife Whose will has always swayed the world, and led it on and upwards to its appointed end.

It is a great argument , it makes one feel angry and helpless. One feels that it is all wrong ; but if God is Almighty, how can it be wrong ? It is utterly logical and consistent; but one can t accept it because one s soul rebels. The truth is, that history drives one to the knowledge that God cannot be absolutely Almighty. It is the Almighty God we are fighting ; He is the soul of Prussianism. I want to kill Him. That is what I m here for. I want to kill the Almighty God and tear Him from His throne. It is Him we are really fighting against. I would gladly die to kill the idea of the Almighty God Who drives men either to cruelty or atheism. This war is no mere national struggle, it is a war between two utterly incompatible visions of God. That is what I'm out for. I want to ensure that men do not worship a false God. I want to win the world to the worship of the patient, suffering

Father God revealed in Jesus Christ. But can I find any traces of that God in history ? Yes, I find Him every where.

> History's pages but record One death-grapple in the darkness
> Twixt old systems and the Word. Bight for ever on the
> scaffold, Wrong for ever on the throne, Yet that scaffold sways
> the future, And, behind the dim unknown, Standeth God
> within the shadow, Keeping watch above His own.

God, the Father God of Love, is every where in history, but nowhere is He Almighty. Ever and always we see Him suffering, striving, crucified, but conquering. God is Love. He is the Author of peace and lover of concord, and all true progress is caused by God and moves toward God, the God of Love. Only as we progress toward unity, concord, and co-operation do we really progress at all. The workings of God in history are quite evident and clear. I see the birth of human unity and concord foreshadowed far back in Nature in the union of the mother and the child. I see it spread out into the family, from the family to the clan, and from the clan to the nation, and from the nation to the empire of free nations, and I look forward, and have a perfect rational right to look for ward, to the final victory and a united world. This progress is there, and it is the work of God, but it bears no trace of being the work of an Almighty God. It has been a broken, slow, and painful progress marked by many failures, a Via Dolorosa wet with blood and tears. So far as human unity exists to-day, it is, like all other good things in the world, the result not only of the power but of the pain of God. We see the God of Love in all the splendid dreams of and efforts after brotherhood and unity which have marked the course of human history. All of them splendid failures.

Above all, I see it in the splendid failure of a dream which found birth within the brain of Christ, and has won the enthusiasm and life-long devotion of so many noble souls, the Catholic Church. The Church has always been a failure, like Christ ; but out of its failure it has won the high success. In it we see the God Father Whom Christ revealed struggling, suffering, crucified, but conquering still. Men leave Him for dead, and behold He is alive again. They despise His weakness, and then find His weakness strong. They mock at the folly of the Father Who leads but will not drive, and then come to see the wisdom of that folly

in the end. For the foolishness of God is wiser than man, and His weakness is stronger than our strength. If the Christian religion means anything, it means that God is Suffering Love, and that all real progress is caused by the working of Suffering Love in the world.

If it means anything, it means that progress is made in spite of, and not because of, strife and war. Human strife is not God's method, but His problem a problem that arises from absolute but temporary necessities inherent in the task of creation. Strife and warfare arise from the limitation which the God of Love had to submit to in order to create spiritual personalities worthy to be called His sons. War is the crucifixion of God, not the working of His will. The Cross is not past, but present. Ever and always I can see set up above this world of ours a huge and towering Cross, with great arms stretched out east and west from the rising to the setting sun, and on that Cross my God still hangs and calls on all brave men to come out and fight with evil, and

by their sufferings endured with Him help to lift the world from darkness into light.

Always that cry from the Cross is answered ; but because of sin, and because we are but children yet, it is only very feebly answered. All nations crucify Him, yet all nations desire Him. All men love Him, and yet, manlike, kill the thing they love because He calls for sacrifice. Longing for Him in our hearts, we deny Him in our lives. We are all hypocrites, and our hypocrisy is our salvation. Honesty would damn our souls to hell, be cause it could only be Prussian honesty of the lower standard. If we were perfectly honest now, it would mean that we had lost the vision of the Highest which makes hypocrites of all.

We cannot be Christian, but we must be as Christian as we can. We cannot even be human, but we must be as human as we can. We can t be saints, but we must be sportsmen. It is beyond us to turn the other cheek, but at least we must not hit below the belt. That is the form our hypocrisy must take, and it is the only foundation for future honesty. The laws of war, the Geneva Convention and its pro visions may be intellectual nonsense, but they are spiritual supersense. They have in them the splendid human inconsistency which is the hall-mark of a man, the super-animal who is always a failure, because his destiny is infinitely high. If one aims at the moon one will not score a bull, but neither will one hit a gooseberry bush.

This is the creed of those who worship the God of Suffering Love, and it is the direct contradiction of the creed of those who worship the supreme untroubled God of power. In this creed, which to men looks like weakness, there lies the source of all true strength. This, I believe, is the real creed of the British Army, if only it could cut itself free from all the complications that have arisen from false teaching in the past.

If we were not fighting this war in order to end all war, and with hatred of war in our hearts, it would be for us, as well as our enemies, another utter disgrace. But that is what the heart of the Allies does mean : it means to end war. The heart of the allied nations means it, for the heart of the nations is in their common people, and they all mean it. The heart of the common people knows nothing about God Almighty, except as a puzzle for parsons, but they long for and fight for brother hood and peace, and therefore, consciously or unconsciously, they long for and fight for the suffering Father God of Love revealed in Jesus Christ.

Hurrah for the army of splendid human hypocrites who blaspheme the God they die for and kill the thing they love. Here's one of them blaspheming Christ and helping in a wounded Boche.

Yes, lad, you can get through now. It's fairly quiet. Follow the white tape and it will bring you through. I wonder, could we carry old Fritz ? I bet that foot is giving him what for.

The Hardest Part

IV: God in the Bible

SITTING at the door of the Regimental Aid Post. Time about 4.30 a.m., after a very rough night in the trenches, during which we had many casualties. Among those who were killed outright was a very popular sergeant. In his breast pocket I found a Bible.

I wonder did he read it. It was given him by his wife. Was it for her sake he carried it, or for what he found in it, or both ? " Yes, I'll ave one, sir ; you never know your luck ; it may stop a bullet." I remember that remark when I was distributing New Testaments to men going up the line from Rouen. " I ll ave one, too, so long as you re giving em away. I left my old one at 'ome as a souvenir." Superstition and sentiment, I wonder why she gave it him. Was it superstition ? Was it sentiment ? Or was it because they both found in its pages the beauty and the strength that come of God ? It s no use blinking facts. He was a splendid fellow, but I don t think he knew much about religion. I think he rather despised what he did know as being the refuge of the weak. He was so strong and self-reliant in his strength, but, dear God, he was lovable.

Of course you never know with English men, they are so splendidly shy about serious things ; but on the whole I don't think he did read it. I m sorry, but I don t.

There are thousands of Bibles carried that are not read. That is certain. If you give them out broadcast, that is bound to be so. The Bible, specially the New Testament, has an enormous circulation in the trenches, yet I very rarely come across a man who knows very much about it. I am always surprised and very much pleased when I do.

I find quite common among men a kind of inherited respect for the Bible. They seem to think of it very much as a decent man thinks of his grandmother. It is ancient, and therefore demands respect ; but it is utterly out of date and

The Hardest Part

cannot be taken seriously, except by parsons, who, of course, are not quite ordinary men ; and even the parsons appear to take parts of it nowadays with a grain of salt. There is, in fact, a vague but widespread feeling that the Bible stands discredited and cannot be appealed to for the solution of the doubts and difficulties of modern life.

There are some men who openly ridicule and despise it ; and very often, strange to say, these men appear to have read it quite a lot, in a superficial kind of way. Some of these are not decent men, and some have got beyond the conventional sense of decency and arrived at a sense of righteousness and higher social justice. They despise the Bible as part and parcel of a disreputable past, and hate it because it has been used to bolster up the weakness of a rotten social system.

It is a strange business, but I am not really surprised. The Bible is a queer Book, as queer as life itself. How about myself ? I m a parson, and I've studied it, of course. I study it still ; but do I love it ? Well, parts of it I do revel in them ; parts of it I don't. I get irritated when I have to read out to people in church some of the stories in the Old Testament. I would not mind if they were read out as legends not supposed to be true, though even then some appear to be pointless and not worth reading out. The worst of it is that we have to read them out with out comment, as though we thought them true and valuable. I don t believe that Balaam's ass spoke, or that Jonah lived in a whale s belly, or that the walls of Jericho fell flat. I am bothered about the plagues, of Egypt and the passage of the Red Sea. Then there are the really bad stories. They are bad, because they give a false idea of God, and so are really blasphemous when read as real truth. God hardens Pharaoh s heart and then destroys him because his heart was hard. That is
frankly immoral. There is the man who put out his hand to steady the Ark and was struck dead by the hand of God. What a God ! I love Elisha, but some of the stories about him

and Elijah are in credible and immoral. I think Elisha's treatment of the children that called him " bald pate " showed that he had no sense of humour, and it s a positive disgrace to drag God into it, as if He hadn't any sense of humour either, when He made it. The children were rude and they ought to have been smacked, but to have them eaten up by bears is the limit. I have heard that taken as a lesson in an Infants School. That is real blasphemy. God is not a bogey-man. Elijah calls down fire from heaven to burn up companies of soldiers who were doing their duty. It is impossible, and immoral as well. Of course I don't believe in the truth of the six days creation or the Flood and Noah s ark ; but then, I don't think those pretend to be true : they are just splendid legends containing great truths.

I don't wonder that the ordinary man gets muddled about the Bible, yet I love it, and I find within its covers the finest things in life.

I love it, because for me it fulfils its purpose, and that is how it must be judged upon the whole, like any other book.

What is the purpose of the Book ? Is it a book at all ? Isn t it just a haphazard collection of writings ? No ; it is a book. That is one of the queerest parts about it. It is a collection of writings by all sorts and conditions of men at all sorts and conditions of times, that, by some strange process of natural or supernatural selection, have got together and made a real Book. There is something odd about the evolution of the canon ; something odder, I mean, than there is about the evolution of a cat. Both, of course, are astounding and God-guided ; but if the one is called natural, I should call the other supernatural. Yes, the Bible is a book, because a single purpose runs through it and makes it one. What is that purpose ? I think it is to teach the love of God. That is the aim and object of it all.

Has it on the whole fulfilled that purpose in the past ? Well, speaking broadly, I think the Bible has a wonderful

The Hardest Part

record. Of course, like that of all other human things, it is not a perfect record. The devil has quoted and misquoted the Bible for his own purpose all down the ages. It s a kind of crooked testimony to its power that he should do so. Scripture has been used to support the ghastliest of crimes. " *Tan- tum religio potuits uadere malonem* " (" See thou to what damned deeds Religion draweth men ") is as true of Christianity as it was of Paganism. The Bible has been the cause of cruelty, intolerance, and tyranny. It has helped in the suppression of learning and the persecution of great pioneers, both scientific and political. It has made men call good evil and evil good, and they have often played the beast with texts of Scripture on their lips. The pages of Holy Writ are stained with many a victim s blood. That is the one side, and, on the other, stands a goodly company of real saints in whose eyes there shines the light that never was on land or sea, caught from these same blood-stained pages of the Book. Such is its record.

Is it then inspired ? Well, accurately speaking, an " it " can t be inspired ; you can only inspire a " him." A book can t be inspired ; only its writers can. The real question is, " Was the Bible written by men inspired by God ? " I think it was.

What do you mean by an inspired man ? I mean a man whose spirit has come into direct and conscious communion with the great personal Spirit Who is the final reality of the world. Well, if that is what I mean, and the Bible was written by such men, and collected by such men, doesn't that mean that every part of the Bible is of equal value and of equal truth, since all the writers were in communion with God ? No, it doesn't mean that. These writers were still men, not machines nor yet mere clerks taking down dictation. They were sinful, sensual, stupid men ; men even who were murderers, adulterers, and thieves like David ; but men who, in spite of all that, had come into touch with the highest. When I read my Bible I am talk ing down the ages to men of like passions with myself, and they are trying to tell me about

God, and what He meant to them and to the people of their time. There are all sorts of difficulties which they have to meet before they can get their message home to me.

First of all they have to overcome their own stupidity and their own sin, which weakens and maims their powers of communion with God. They were not miraculously sinless or intellectually perfect men.

Then there is the difficulty of speech. Words are awful things, so strong and yet so very weak. The deepest thoughts can not be said. All great speech, like all great art, is an effort to express the inexpressible. These men were not endowed with miraculously perfect speech.

Finally, they have to meet my stupidity and my sin before I get the message. Even if an absolutely perfect revelation could be written, I would not have the purity of heart or the clearness of mind necessary to understand it.

With all these difficulties to meet and overcome, do you wonder that their message is not perfect or perfectly expressed ?

When men criticise the Bible they tend to take all its shining beauty and illuminating truth for granted, and to pounce upon the faults and falsehoods. Their criticism has no basis of genuine appreciation. Why do men display this tendency ? Why do they allow the mystery of evil to obliterate the mystery of good ? Because, I believe, they have at the back of their minds this impossible conception of an omnipotence which knows no difficulties and has no obstacles to overcome. They think that if the Bible is inspired by God Almighty it ought to be perfect and accurate in every detail of truth, and all parts of it equally perfect, since God had only to touch men s lips and Truth, with words wherein to express it, would flow like rivers from their mouths.

There is in the Bible no trace of such omnipotence ; it is as foreign to the real spirit of the Bible as it is to any real life. One cannot find God Almighty in the Bible any more than we find Him in Nature or in history. We see in the Bible, as we see everywhere else, the patient, persistent suffering spirit of love and beauty at war with awful and incomprehensible necessities, and slowly conquering them.

The Bible is not merely the history of God's self-revelation to man, it is the history of the making of man capable of receiving the revelation ; and it is as slow, as chequered, and as painful a process as the progress of man in any other department of life has been. The whole Bible is a Book of Genesis, and is full of the travail pains of the eternal love. It is not only our sin which we, at any rate partly, will, but our ignorance and stupidity which we do not will at all, that makes, and always has made, love suffer in His work.

By stupidity I mean the lack of imagination, sympathy, and intuition which a man cannot help, because it is a defect in his general make-up so to speak. A man can almost always help being a knave, but millions of men are born fools. It is one of the awful necessities inherent in God s task of creation that He has to suffer fools gladly, and it is no small part of the burden which He has to bear. It is this tragedy of human stupidity which lies behind the first word from the Cross " Father, forgive them, they know not what they do."

This necessary stupidity, which is due to the fact of our incompleteness, for we are only beginnings at the best, is the inevitable burden which the Creator had to take upon Himself. It could not be avoided. We make this burden heavier by adding to our natural stupidity our sin; that is, our deliberate and wilful misuse of the powers we possess. Part of God s sorrow is absolutely necessary, and part is only necessary because we will it to be so. It is absolutely necessary that God should create and suffer in creation, we make it necessary that He should also redeem and suffer in redemption. The Bible is the history of God's agony in creation and redemption. It shows how painfully and slowly God managed to overcome the obstacles of man's stupidity and sin, and show him the truth which is eternal life in

Christ. The life and death of Christ are the epoch-making events in that great story of Divine patience and pain, and in the light of the Cross all history becomes luminous. In the Cross God gathers up all history into a moment of time, and shows to us the meaning of it. It is the act in time which reveals to us the eternal activity of suffering and redeeming love all down the ages.

Every nation has its Bible, and that Bible is its history. It is only the fact that the Hebrews were possessed of unique religious genius that makes their Bible take precedence of all others in the world, and it was that which made it inevitable that the Incarnation should take place among them. In the light of the Hebrew Bible all other Bibles can be read and understood, since it is the same God Who inspires the writers of them all, the only difference being one of degree.

It would be too much to attempt to describe in detail the slow and painful progress of the knowledge of God among the Jews which is revealed to us in the pages of Holy Writ. One would want one's library, and I have only a Boche helmet and a water-bottle, but the main stages are clear.

They started from non-moral polytheism like all other peoples, but were apparently the first people in the world to discover that God was good and demanded goodness from His children. They did not doubt the existence of other gods, but were convinced that their God was good, and that because He was good He was superior to all other gods, and would in the end conquer them, and make His chosen people lords of all the world.

The Jews, however, were not a conquering, but an often conquered people, and their faith in Jehovah's invincibility was sorely tried. Disaster after disaster crowded in upon them, and in this furnace of affliction they learned a higher truth. There was only one God in all the world, and that God good. He was the supreme Almighty Sovereign of the earth and sky, and all things were according to His will. The cause of all their disasters was the hand of God punishing them for their sins. Famine, fire, pestilence, disease, and war were the weapons that God used to drive His people back to Him and His laws.

It was God Who brought the stranger from the north or south to devastate the land. Caught between two mighty empires, the Belgium of the ancient world, they suffered horribly, and brutal conquerors destroyed their homes and killed their children before their eyes. Their noblest teachers interpreted their disasters to them as the working of the Almighty Righteous God visiting His people with punishment for their sins, and every fresh disaster as a stronger call to repentance. His anger was not turned away, but His arm was stretched out still. Nevertheless, they did discern that behind the anger of God there was compassion and love. If
God chastised them it was for their good. These great teachers had dim vision of the Fatherhood of God which Christ perfectly revealed. By sheer genius of spiritual intuition, and not like the Greeks by long process of reason, they came to the truth that creation was a universe ruled by One Supreme Power Who was perfectly righteous and perfectly loving, and they believed Him also to be absolutely all-powerful.

This great faith they clung to in the teeth of awful difficulty. They saw the righteous forsaken and down-trodden, and the ungodly in great prosperity and flourishing like a green bay tree. The Old Testament is full of the pain of this problem of evil which faces us to-day. If God be a righteous and a loving God, and if all disasters and diseases are His punishments for sin, why do they fall so heavily on the innocent, and why do the wicked prosper ? This is the sorrow of the Psalms and the pathetic puzzle discussed in the Book of Job. No solution was forthcoming. It was an utter mystery.

> It is higher than heaven ; what canst thou do ?
> It is deeper than hell ; what canst thou know ?

The Hardest Part

Job is faced in the end with a vision of the power of God which strikes him dumb and brings him to his knees, and the drama ends with an artificial solution in which Job is restored to all his riches and prosperity. The ending refuses to face the facts of the lifelong suffering of the best and noblest men, and the apparent injustice of it, and goes back to the faith that God does punish the guilty and reward the innocent in this world.

There is the beginning of a higher vision which just glimmers through the darkness for men like Hosea and the writer of the fifty-third chapter of Isaiah. They grope after but fail to grasp the truth that there is not only love and anger, but also bitter sorrow in God s heart, and the writer of the great chapter sees that when the innocent suffer for the guilty, such suffering is a majestic and adorable thing, and has a power to redeem from sin beyond the power of punishment. It is a marvellous advance in knowledge, and it comes very near the real truth.

But God is still left Almighty and Serene. He inflicts but does not suffer sorrow. It is He that afflicts the suffering servant and lays on him the iniquity of all. He sits on His throne and receives the intercession of the suffering servant for sinners who deserve punishment. The Prophet sees the majesty of suffering love, but does not dare to carry it into the heart of God. He was not ready yet for that, but was getting near. The Old Testament closes with the vision of the Almighty God, half King, half Father, Who punishes the wicked and rewards the innocent in this life, and leaves the mystery of innocent suffering still unsolved in pathetic and painful blackness against the absolute omnipotence of God.

Then Christ comes. He reproduces in every living line the picture of the suffering servant in Isaiah, but He claims to be not the servant but the Son of God, the image of the Father, and one with Him in a perfect unity. He carries innocent suffering into the heart of God, and explains its power to redeem as the power of the suffer ing Father of Love.

There is about Him no trace of human royalty, there is no pomp or pageantry, and no show of force where with to drive men to His will. He comes in weakness, the weakness of God which is stronger than men.

History of course repeats itself. The glimmer of truth that had broken upon Isaiah had not penetrated to the minds of the people or their leaders, except a very few. The common people hear him gladly, for there is the magic of perfect love in His words, but they want to make Him an earthly king and arm Him with a sword. That must be His place if He is the Messiah of God. He refuses it with a shudder. He will not touch the sceptre, and He will not wield the sword. God is not like that. He transforms the whole idea of kingship, and reinterprets it in terms of love and not of material power. Because He is a King the King therefore He must suffer, must be mocked, spit on, crucified, and tortured as God has been all down the ages. But also because He is the King he must rise again and go on suffering and striving until His task shall be complete.

God is like that. God is suffering, but triumphant, love. The final revelation of God in Christ Who suffered, died, and rose again to go on suffering in His Church, finally tears the Almighty God armed with pestilence and disease from His throne, and reveals the patient, suffering God of love Who endures an agony unutterable in the labour of creation, but endures on still for love s sake to the end.

It is the final truth, but it was miles beyond the world of His day, and it is miles beyond us still.

The tragedy of man s inveterate stupidity continues. The crown that Christ rejected here on earth, the throne of material power which He refused to mount, are given Him in heaven. Men were ashamed of the Cross, ; and they could not see it as God s real throne. They invented the so-called "glorified Christ," Who, with all His sorrows ended and all His struggles won, ascends to share the throne of God Almighty and enjoy His perfect peace.

The Hardest Part

White-robed angels stand about Him bowing to His least command, shouts of triumph greet His entrance, the mighty gates lift up their heads and the King of glory enters in. All the pageantry of earthly power, all the pomp of courts and kings which He on earth refused, are used to make Him beautiful, forsooth, Who needs no robes of beauty but His sorrow and His love.

Christ is clothed in that omnipotence which has been all down the ages the veil that hid the real glory of the suffering God of love. But the Cross remained. It made its mark, and men could not forget. It is of course God s real throne, the throne of love that lifts Him up, and draws all men to Him at last. The power of the Cross is the power of God. It is not past, but ever present. God has no other, and needs no other, glory but the glory of the Cross the glory of suffering, striving, and unconquerable love. This glorified Christ in regal robes is a degraded Christ reft of real majesty ; these baubles are not worthy of the King. The true God is naked, bloody, wounded, and crowned with thorns, tortured, but triumphant in His love. He is God, and when men s eyes once see Him they must worship Him. He possesses them body and soul, and will never let them go. He is coming to His own to-day. The furnace of this world war is burning out the dross of dead conventions from the Christian creed, and showing up the pure gold of the Cross.

All men are learning to worship patient, suffering love, and the muddy bloody hero of the trenches is showing us Who is the real King. The darkness is being cleared away, and men at last are growing proud of the Cross. Beside the wounded tattered soldier who totters down to this dressing-station with one arm hanging loose, an earthly king in all his glory looks paltry and absurd. I know nothing in my real religion of the Almighty God of power. I only see God in Christ, and these men have shown me—*Him.*

I have seen in them His glory, glory as of the Only Begotten of the Father, full of grace and truth.

I am sure of this God. I know Him. I love Him. I worship Him. I would die for Him and be glad.

Doc, I've been dreaming. I'm going up the line now. How s that lad inside ? Dead ? O God, comfort his mother. I must bury him at once. He was an only son.

V: God and Democracy

IN a tent two days after a big battle. A battalion parade had just been held. The thanks of the Commander-in-Chief had been conveyed to the troops for their gallantry in the recent action, and parade finished with " God save the King."

I never was thrilled by " God save the King " before. As a rule it leaves me cold ; to-day it sent a tingling down my spine and gave me a lump in my throat. I wonder why. I suppose I am a bit upset really; hell is bad for the nerves. The parade was pretty awful too, so many splendid chaps absentees ; it gets on one s nerves. I suppose I am a bit windy. We are all in for it again the day after tomorrow, and there will be more absentees. " The King " sounded so dauntless and determined. It seemed like the song of a thousand martyrs on their road to death. *Morituri te salutamus* business, only in a nobler cause. It thrilled one like a great confession of faith. And yet, if there is anything certain, it is that " God save the King " is not the British Army's confession of faith. Conventionally it may be ; really it is nothing of the kind. I suppose there are a thousand reasons, good and bad, why these dear chaps come out to fight.

Some came because they were not going to stand bullying, and they regard the Prussian as a bully. Some fight because
they think liberty as they know it and understand it is at stake ; others because they are Englishmen, and they are not going to see their side defeated if they can help it. Some enlisted because their pals did, or their girl said they ought. But I doubt whether any fight as did the Cavaliers of Charles I because they think the English monarchy a divine institution.

The divine right of kings is an idea as foreign to the British soldier's mind as the infallibility of the Pope. To him it is purely a matter of expediency whether you have a king with crown or president with a top hat. He regards them both as public servants, and respects them for the work they do. The British peoples would not tolerate for an instant the pretensions of a king who took himself seriously as an absolute monarch. They will have any king but Caesar. To us the Kaiser could not be anything but a bad joke.

No; if the B.E.F. were to make a confession of faith, it would be a vague and sketchy thing, and I doubt if the King would have a place in it at all. It would all centre round the ideas of Democracy and Freedom. Everywhere I find among the men of the army that this is the one great thing that touches them and rouses real enthusiasm. They do believe in Democracy. They are not quite sure what it means, but whatever it means, they believe in it. They believe intensely that every man has a right to a voice in the government of his country. This conviction is the only one of an ultimate kind that I find common and intense throughout the British Army. If they have any religion, it is centered in this idea of Democratic Freedom. This is their faith, vague and shadowy, but enormously powerful and big with mighty issues, good and evil, for the days that are to come.

I was driven to this truth about the British soldier by my wanderings as a preacher throughout the bases and the armies in the field, and I was driven against my will, for, in many ways, the prospect frightens me.

Any form of democracy is bound to throw such an enormous weight of responsibility upon the ordinary average man, and he, splendid fellow as he is, seems to be much more alive to his rights than to his responsibilities in the free democracy which is to be.

This much is certain. The pomp and pageantry of kings, the glamour that surrounds a throne, the outward symbols of royalty have lost all power of appeal to the ordinary man. He looks upon them as he looks upon a Lord Mayor's show, as quaint and picturesque relics of antiquity, that give pleasure on a holiday, but have nothing to do with the serious business of life. The sentiment of passionate loyalty to a king does not exist among the rank and file of the army.

It is hard to part with it without regret, for this passion has a glorious history, but a history full of pathos too. Alas ! the record of the race of kings is stained with many crimes. Too often have the kings betrayed and traded on the loyalty and faith of men. They have used them as a stalking horse to further their intrigues to purely selfish ends. They have used the doctrine that the king can do no wrong as a public licence to misuse their power. The treachery of kings has had its inevitable result, and men have ceased to trust in them. Even those who still hold that a benevolent despotism is the best form of government will add with a sigh," given the benevolent despot," and he is so very rarely given.

The average man does not read history, yet history lives in him; each one of us is history incarnate, and history has killed blind trust in kings.

Of course this is not the only, or the chief, cause of the coming of Democracy. The power behind that coming appears to be the power that lies behind the gradual development of man. It is as near to being inevitable as anything can be in a world of men and women whose wills are partly free. In the days when men s light was largely darkness and ignorance was the common lot of most, when they were babes in brain power, they could be treated as such and ruled as such.

States could be ruled as a father rules a family of small children, who cannot question or dispute his right to rule and punish as he wills. When, however, the children grow up and learn, the form of family government must change, unless it is to ruin the children. So with states. If we seriously wish to stop the coming of Democracy, we must at once, and first of all, abolish free and compulsory education.

The Hardest Part

I have met men who said they would do this if they could, because modern elementary education does more harm than good, giving us that little knowledge which is so dangerous a thing. I think it is only talk. It is easy to see the dangers of the Primary School education, but there is only one way of abolishing it, and that is to put some better, higher form of education in its place. Talk about the abolition of education is just talk for talking s sake. It may turn a point in an argument, but it has no relation to facts. We are going to have more education, not less or none at all. In order to be effective at all, opponents of Democracy ought to be passive resisters and refuse to pay their rates. They would then be splendidly consistent, and to most men irresistibly comic.

No; education has come to stop, and the immediate result of it, however in complete, is to develop in man the critical faculty. Criticism is easier than construction, and comes first. It is the critical faculty of the people that destroys their faith in kings absolute kings, or indeed in absolute anythings or anybodies. It has been and will be found increasingly difficult to protect anything or anybody from criticism. As the minds of men develop they become less and less afraid, and more determined to prove all things and hold fast only that which is true. Everywhere this tendency can be traced in history. Combined with a deep and pathetic longing for an absolute authority and an in fallible guide, there is this critical faculty which prevents us from resting satisfied with false absolutes. Men tried an in fallible Church, and the critical faculty tore it to pieces after the Renaissance; they tried an infallible Bible, and the nineteenth - century science cast it into a den of critics whose mouths could not be closed. They have tried infallible monarchies again and again, and seen them torn to bits. What France did in the Revolution, what Portugal did yesterday, Russia is doing to-day. All the energy of effort that has been used to protect Church or Bible or Czar from criticism has been in vain, and must be in vain, unless you abolish education.

The Roman Church still tries to keep her absolute authority alive and to strangle the critical faculty of men for men s own good. She is, however, rather like a desperately conscientious policeman endeavouring to stop the march of an army terrible with banners, and she is left, as he would be left, with the helmet of salvation on the back of her head, furiously waving the baton of pomposity (having mislaid the sword of the Spirit) and wildly calling upon an incorrigibly progressive humanity to turn back under threat of the Divine dis pleasure. It is pathetically hopeless !

There is a party, too, of the Church in England which desires and strives to regain the absolute coercive authority of the Church. They are even more pathetic. They are like special constables faced with an army, as powerless as the policeman, but without his dignity, for the great religious policeman is really dignified even in the invidious position in which he is placed.

It is all wrong. You cannot, and of course ought not to, protect anything or anybody from criticism, not even God. It is really all part of the same pathetic fallacy which has been the root of intolerance and persecution all down the ages the fallacy that the human soul can be driven and compelled. It is false reverence which seeks to protect truth from attack. True reverence only begins when criticism has done its work. The same error which made the inquisitors burn men for speaking against the Church, and made monarchs burn men for speaking against the throne, makes men threaten with future torments those who speak against the creeds. It is all futile. God invites criticism, asks for it, pleads for it. He challenges us with mysteries, and lures us on by mighty questions to find the living truth.

The faculty of faith is not meant to kill the faculty of criticism and the instinct of curiosity, but rather to keep them keen and alive, and prevent them dying of despair. Faith is the mark of those who seek and keep on seeking, who ask and keep on asking, who knock and keep on knocking, until the door is opened. The passive weak-kneed taking of everything on trust which is often represented as faith, is a travesty of its truth. True faith is the most active, positive, and powerful of all virtues. It means that a man, having come into spiritual communion with that great personal Spirit Who lives and works behind the universe, can trust Him, and trusting Him can use all his powers of body, mind, and spirit to co-operate with Him in the great purpose of perfection ; it means that the man of faith will be the man of science in its deepest, truest sense, and will never cease from asking questions, never cease from seeking for the reason that lies behind all mysteries. There are, of course, a thousand things that are at present super-rational : not contrary to but beyond reason ; but that fact does not call us to cease from reasoning, but rather bids us reason more and more carefully. Faith is not the anchor but the lodestar of the intellect ; it bids it follow, and it keeps it true.

The doctrine that the king can do no wrong has been used all down the ages to stifle political criticism, and so stunt social progress. It has been used to kill the hopes and aspirations of the people, and keep them from seeking the better land to which their instincts urged them on. Absolute monarchy has been used to stifle the divine discontent which is the hall-mark of humanity.

The doctrine that God can do no wrong has been used in exactly the same way. God's will has been a shibboleth for those who wished to bolster up the existing social order. God is Almighty, and God can do no wrong, and therefore, whatever is, is right.

> The rich man in his castle,
> The poor man at his gate.
> God made them high or lowly
> And ordered their estate.

The Hardest Part

So we sang with childish lips, and so we were taught and believed until we learned in the school of the world that the rich man often not always, but often entered his castle by filthy ways, paved with human miseries and wet with human blood, and that it was often not God but whisky that put the poor man at his gate.

Once the eyes of man are opened to the power and persistence of evil in the world, this pious or impious fatalism becomes impossible; and when men have learned to hate evil with all their hearts, it becomes not only impossible but repulsive and disgusting.

It is this repulsive fatalism, springing from the doctrine of the absolute God, that has embittered many of the noblest social and scientific pioneers against the Christian religion, and embitters them still. It makes a man who has studied modern poverty mad with rage to be told that Christ blessed the poor, and said they would always be with us, and that there fore the social distinctions, as they exist at present, are the will of God.

This vision of God as an Almighty Monarch swaying the world to His will has ruined the religion of some of the noblest souls, and has been productive of evil all down the ages.

God sat upon His throne armed with poverty, pestilence, disease, war, and sudden death in every form, and with these weapons vindicated His majesty upon earth. When a plague of some filthy disease swept over a country, and men lay writhing with pain from some incurable malady, it was the hand of God, smiting them for their good.

God sent these evils, and God alone could remove them, and so men must betake themselves to prayer. If a volcanic eruption destroyed a village, it was God's vengeance on the sinful inhabitants; the Titanic struck an iceberg, it was God's punishment for the luxury of the dining rooms. Nay, according to a dignitary of the Anglican Communion, if a

European war breaks out, it is God s judgment on the drink bill of England.

From this vision of God the reason of man has revolted. They have determined that these things are evil, and must be abolished. Faced with plagues they have deliberately turned from prayers to sanitation, with marvellous success. Faced with disease they have rejected resignation to the will of God and have betaken them selves to scientific research with great results. Practically speaking, men have decided that there is much in the world that is not God s will, but is wrong, and must be abolished. Theoretical religion has lagged behind, and hung on still to the Almighty Monarch to Whom all things do bow and obey. The result is that many of the finest practical people have no use for religion.

The pioneers of social betterment and scientific enlightenment have found them selves opposed or damned with faint praise by the people of God, and so have forsaken God, the conventional God, as decent men were bound to do. So comes about the awful state of things that God s foes are often those of His own household narrow- minded, ignorant, conventional Christians while His firmest friends are too often found among men outside the pale who do not call upon His Name.

That God can do no wrong is indeed the truest of all truth ; but that does not mean that there is no wrong, but that wrong is against God's will, that He hates it, that it thwarts and tortures Him, that He is constantly and actively striving to over come it, and is overcoming it, and finally that He calls upon us, not for passive resignation, but for fierce and strenuous opposition in His Name.

I believe in God the Father Almighty is not a statement of fact but a confession of faith. It does not declare the existence of an absolute Almighty Monarch Who sits upon a throne and moves the world by His nod: it professes our faith in suffering, striving, but all-conquering spirit of perfect love, Who through pain and tribulation, which torture Him, now is working His purpose of perfection out. The first clause of the Creed is not a cold, theological statement of fact, it is a warrior s battle-cry. It is said by the soldiers of God, standing at attention with their faces turned toward God s altar and the dawn of better days.

In those splendid words we declare our faith that the victory of God is as sure and surer than the rising of to-morrow s sun. God is suffering His agony now, but the day will surely come when His agony and ours will be ended, and we shall sing our song of praise to the triumphant God of Love.

The day of the absolute monarch is passing in politics passing in tears and terror. We are burning that effigy in the hell flames of this cruel war, whose worm dieth not and whose fire is not quenched. His day is done, and with him must pass all the metaphors and symbols, both symbolic words and symbolic ideas, which are drawn from the throne of earthly tyrants and applied to God.

We must learn afresh what spirit we are of. When the Sons of Thunder called on Christ to vindicate His majesty by burning the Samaritans with fire from heaven, Christ rebuked them, saying that they knew not the Spirit of God, Who came to save and not destroy ; and as He rebuked them, so would He rebuke us for our conceptions of God.

One of the ablest and most energetic of our bishops at the outbreak of the war started a campaign, the watchword of which was " The majesty of God." God was King, and by the horrors of Pentecostal calamity strove to turn men back to Him. Men had neglected His worship, despised His commandments, rejected His Kingdom, and this was the vindication of His majesty.

At the time, staggered by the immensity of the evil, I simply did not think ; I submitted. Now, after three years of it, I believe that this teaching is liable to be utterly misunderstood, and does but give occasion to the enemies of the Lord to blaspheme. Never again, I believe, will men bow down and worship this majestic tyrant who sits upon a throne and wields as weapons pestilence, disease, and war. Such a vision of God rouses in the best of men, not reverence, but revolt ; not loyalty, but contempt ; not love, but bitter hatred.

The Church lives on its vision of God. No perfection of organization, no multiplication of effort, is of any real good apart from vision. I believe that if she goes forth to meet the world armed with the vision of God upon a throne, she will die. If she goes forth in any power but the power of the Cross she will die.

She lives and works now, so far as she has real life and energy, and thank God she still has much of both, because she holds up before men for their worship and adoration, not God Almighty seated on a throne, the Lord of all power and might, but Jesus Christ, naked, bleeding, but unbeaten on the Cross, the Lord of all courage and love. Though we do our best to cloud the splendid sorrow of this vision by frantic efforts to reconcile it with the serene, omnipotent, passionless monarch on a throne, still through the clouds of our stupidity the Cross finds way into the heart of man, because it is God, the living God, Whose light is shining there.

Men, I believe, have done for ever with crowns of gold. They do not respect, but despise them. Most decent men, looking upon the tattered, muddy, bloody khaki of a procession of wounded that comes in after a battle would say, " Solomon in all his glory was not arrayed like one of these." In their hearts all true men worship one God the naked, wounded, bloody, but unconquered and unconquerable Christ. This is the God for Whom the heart of , democracy is longing, and after Whom it is blindly, blunderingly, but earnestly groping.

The heart of the common people is near to the heart of Christ in its view of royalty. "The kings of the Gentiles," He said, "exercise lordship over them ; and they that wield this power are called benefactors. But it shall not be so with you ; but he that is greatest among you shall be as the younger ; and he that leadeth as he that doth serve."

So Christ pronounced the doom of Kaiser-ism, and it is being wrought out. No superiority of breeding or of brains, no pre-eminence of social position, no power of wealth, appeals to us apart from service. An idle duke is frankly disreputable, and infinitely inferior to a working dustman. The dustman may perhaps die a pauper, but that is nothing to the disgrace of living as a parasite. A man possessed of great powers must be either a devoted public servant or a damned nuisance. Service is the only thing we can respect, and suffering service is the only that we can crown.

We have come to see the hollow mockery of power that is not love. This is the truth which is dawning rapidly upon the heart and head of modern democracy. It is, of course, only a great ideal still. Demos still has idols, and there its danger lies. We still bow down and worship the gods of wealth and position. Fine clothes still cover as great a multitude of sins as charity. To be respectable still means to have a banking account. We have amongst us still, snobs and sycophants, to whom a title is a real triumph and a coronet a halo that outshines the glory of a saint. Snobbery and servility of this kind are common in every class, commoner perhaps among the common people than they themselves are ready to allow. Nevertheless, this is not our real faith. We may still worship idols, but in our hearts we despise them, and despise ourselves for worshipping them. The only thing we can respect, and remain self-respecting, is loving service. The worship of idols is rooted in fear, and the progress of man is the conquest of fear. Perfect love casteth out fear. So, at last, the great suffering, striving God of service and of love is coming to His own, and as He comes into His own, so the High and Mighty Potentate, King of kings and Lord of lords, Almighty God, powerful, passionless, and serene, is being deposed from His throne in the hearts of men, and in His place there standeth one amongst us Whom we knew not,

The Hardest Part

with bloody brow and pierced hands, majestic in His nakedness, superb in His simplicity, the King whose crown is a crown of thorns. He is God.

His coronation by mankind is drawing nearer through the clouds of battle smoke that hide the inner thoughts of men in the Europe of to-day. He is revealing Himself to men out there in a thousand different ways. He is calling to His service men of every sort, and among them many to whom the name of Christ, and the idea of the Christian Church, mean nothing or worse than nothing. Men are turning to God in Christ, even as they curse the Christian God. They do not, and will not, believe in the monarch on the throne ; they do, and will, believe in the Servant on the Cross.

"Every inch a king." So the Kaiser was described by a journalist who saw him at a great military review before the war. Power perfectly personified he was, with his thousand different uniforms and end less royal robes, mounted on his charger, reviewing the greatest and most perfect army in the world. An impressive personality. A wretched withered anachronism, all the more wretched, and all the more withered to us now that we know what he meant. We despised him when we thought he stood for nought but empty pomp and show of power. We despise him much more now we know that he stands for the brutal reality of loveless power. We despise him, as free men despise all tyrants. We can no longer interpret ultimate reality in the terms of absolute monarchy if we are to reach the heart of men. Christ has come so far into His own that He has slain Caesar. The danger is lest the people go out and away toward Christ beyond the Church, and she proves helpless to aid them with the problems they must face. The British Demos is astoundingly Christian, but it is exposed to awful dangers as it advances in freedom and takes up the inevitable burden of responsibility.

A free democracy must have a living religion if it is to live. I love the Church of England, and am proud to be her priest, but, O God of sorrow, love, and service, open her eyes that she may see and live. The people perish now, to spite their wonderful hold on truth, because they want a guide to lead them higher still and the Church lags behind, and sits upon a fence, because her vision of God is dim.

Perhaps, after all, I ought to be thrilled by " God save the King." Our English kings are public servants now. The King of the British is a monarch of free men. A patient, painstaking, public servant upon whom great burdens of responsibility rest. If any king survives it will be ours, for he is very nearly a "Christian king." The crown of our British kings is a crown of golden thorns. Perhaps our English " God save the King " is a fit song for the Army of the Free. I think I will always love it more since I have heard it sung by men who stood at attention with death behind them and death before.

The Hardest Part

VI: God and Prayer

IN the trenches during a heavy bombardment. It lasted over two hours. We could do nothing but sit still and wait. A sergeant on one side of me swore great oaths and made jokes by turns. A man some where on the other side kept praying aloud, in a broken and despairing kind of way, shivering out piteous supplications to God for protection and safety.

I wish that chap would chuck that praying. It turns me sick. I d much rather he swore like the sergeant. It s disgusting, somehow. It isn t religion, it s cowardice. It isn t prayer, it s wind. I d like to shut him up. He probably seldom, if ever, prayed before, and now he substitutes prayer for pluck. I wouldn't mind if he d pray for pluck, but it s all for safety. I hate this last resort kind of religion ; it s blasphemy. The decent men all despise it. Look at the sergeant s face. That other chap keeps banging into his mind a connection between Christ and cowardice. That s where the blasphemy comes in. There is not, and there cannot be, any connection between Christ and cowardice. I wonder who is to blame for this miserable caricature of Christian prayer. Is it the chap himself? Is it just common blue funk, or are his teachers partly to blame, who lead him to suppose that God could and would hearken to this piteous wailing ? I wonder is there something wrong in the way men learn to pray?

"Whatsoever ye ask in My name, I will do it for you." It is a sweeping kind of promise, and easily misunderstood. Lots of Christians seem to think it means that prayer is a kind of magic cheque upon the bank of Heaven, only needing the formal endorsement with Christ s name to make it good for anything.

Of course it does not come off. Millions of such cheques are dishonoured every day. When the war broke out there was a regular run upon the bank of God, and our churches were thronged with distracted people wav ing cheques for protection, duly endorsed "through Jesus Christ our Lord," and still the German host swept on and trampled helpless Belgium underfoot. I suppose there must have been millions of German and Austrian prayer cheques presented at the same time. They soon got sick of it of course, and fell away. In a dim way they realised that it was useless, and a waste of time. I believe we parsons were, and are still, much to blame. We have not told people the truth about prayer for fear of hurting their feelings or discouraging them in their prayers. We went on the theory that any kind of prayer is better than no prayer at all. A chaplain said that to me the other day. "Don't discourage last-resort religion ; it is better than no religion at all." I don t agree. It s worse than no religion; it s a base and superstitious form of idolatry.

I think there can be little doubt that we have encouraged this magic idea by the monotonous and formal ending of our prayers with the sacred Name, as if the name had power in itself. Of course prayer in Christ s name means prayer in Christ s spirit. The greatest of all prayers does not contain the Name, but is drenched with the spirit. What is Christ s spirit ? In a word, " heroism." God and my duty first a long way first. God s will above and beyond all other things. My pals and other people second. Myself and my own desires last, and a long way last, almost nowhere. That is Christ. Now what s this poor devil thinking about ? Not his duty, not his pals; he s forgotten all about them. His whole mind is filled with one idea ; the safety of his own skin. Well, don't be hard on him. Perhaps he has a wife and a kiddie at home, like your Patrick. I don t want to be hard, but I must be Christian. Christ said, " He that hateth not father and mother," and other fierce, hard sentences. He made it plain that in big things, when God's will was made clear to us, we must put Him and duty out away beyond even the wife and kiddies. It may be hard, but it is Christian. This is not prayer at all.

Cowardice has turned it into sin. It is sin, not prayer. To think of one's own skin now, to pray for one's own safety, is sin. There is no such thing as selfish prayer. There is no such thing as prayer which does not put God first. That is the essence of it. That is the spirit. The name without the spirit is as futile as the mumbo-jumbo of a conjuror. This chaps prayer is much more sinful than the sergeant s swears. There is love in the sergeant s blasphemy. He may not be thinking about God, but he is thinking about his platoon. He may not be a Christian, but at any rate he s not a coward. I suppose he has the ordinary brave man's idea about death and danger. He s a fatalist. "If it s coming, it s coming; if it ain't, it ain't; and any ow, I can 'elp it." That s what he d say. " If the bullet or the shell is made that has my name on it, then I m for it any ow." It isn't the Christian way. It isn t the noblest way. But it s a brave way. It resists the temptation of fear. It crushes down this cursed terror that takes your spirit by the throat and drives it into selfish cowardice the cowardice that will not let you do your job with all your heart and soul, and think of comrades first. It means, at any rate, that the spirit holds its own even if it can't attack.

Of course the Christian spirit rips through that and goes out beyond it. It is not merely fatalistic in that dull sort of way ; it is utterly and joyfully reckless. Danger doesn't matter, death doesn't matter ; only God and the job matter at all. The Christian spirit despises death and laughs at danger, if they be on the road where duty leads. It does not merely face the shadow of death, it sees through it into the life beyond ; it does not merely withstand fear, it tramples it underfoot, it kills it, and leaps out to find the courage of the Cross. The Christian spirit is the spirit of positive, powerful, and infectious heroism. It is not content with refusing to let pals down, it seeks to encourage, inspire, and uplift them. It is the spirit of that supremest kind of moral courage which includes physical courage, and trans forms the splendour of the bull-dog into the splendour of the Christ. The British Army is full of splendid bull-dogs like this old swearing sergeant, and they make it glorious. But, dear God, what an army we would have if every soldier prayed, and, through prayer, caught up the spirit of the Christ ! An army of British Christians would take the Kaiser in its stride, and beat the devil himself.

I see Gethsemane ; I always see it these days. Christ Himself was once in danger of losing that splendid spirit. He is faced with the agony of the Cross. The sickening feeling that men, who have stood as we stand now, know something of sweeps over Him. It is worse for Him ; how much worse we cannot altogether understand. He was alone for one thing ; that made it worse. God, how I hate being alone with darkness and the fear of death. One pal makes all the difference. He had no chance either ; there was no hope of a blighty one, and then home. It is certain death, and certain torture. He is in the grip of terror. We see Him alone in the garden, praying. Three times the horror of the Cross wrings from His lips the human cry, " If it be possible, let this cup pass from Me." Let Me off, O God ; let Me off, I cannot bear it. That is not His prayer, that is what He is praying against, that is the expression of the terror He has to fight. But each time the prayer follows, the real prayer, with power that receives immediate answer : " Nevertheless, Thy will be done." That is the real prayer. They ruined it all for me as a child ; they told me that God's will was the Cross. God wished Christ to be crucified ; He wished Judas to be a traitor, Pilate a coward, the priests to be fiends, and the crowd to be cruel and fickle-hearted. It was all part of His plan. Of course that is impossible. God cannot plan treachery and murder. They told me that when Christ realised that His prayer could not be answered, He meekly bowed His head to God's plan, and said, " Thy will be done." The cry of agony was the prayer, and "Thy will be done" an act of meek submission. It is the topsy-turvy kind of interpretation that arises from the Al mighty Monarch on the Throne idea of God, Who wills both good and evil. But it is madness. God could not will the

Cross. It must have been utterly abhorrent to Him. God s will for Christ was that He should live the perfect life, bear witness to the final truth, and bear the torch of perfect love undimrned through everything. That was God's will, and Christ s work ; and if it was to be done, it must mean that the Cross be carried, and all it meant endured, to the very end. That was necessary because of sin. So in His agony Christ prays " Thy will be done." The prayer is immediately answered. The angel of God appears to comfort Him. Terror dies within His soul, hesitation disappears, and with His battle prayer upon His lips, " Thy will be done," He goes out from the garden in the majesty of manhood to bear such witness to His truth, to live in death so fine a life, that He becomes the light in darkness of every age, and the deathless hope of a dying world.

The great truth is that " Thy will be done " is the real prayer of Gethsemane. It is the prayer, and not an afterthought of sad submission in case God cannot answer the prayer to be let off.

Too often we model our prayers upon the false interpretation of Gethsemane. Our prayers are too often either a wail of agony or a kind of indent upon God for supplies to meet our needs, with " Thy will be done " put in at the end in case God cannot take away the pain we plead against or grant us the supplies we need. " Thy will be done " ceases to be the great prayer, and becomes the necessary apology for praying.

It becomes an act of passive submission instead of an act of positive and powerful aspiration. Much of our war prayer in churches at home, and much of our peace prayer too, is rendered futile by this false conception. We parsons are to blame. We have been kind to be cruel because we were afraid of being cruel to be kind ; we have failed to be Christian because we tried to be kinder than Christ. We have not called upon our people for heroism in their prayers. We have accepted the lower standard, and excused it by saying that it is human. Of course it is human, but religion must be more than human or else it must be vain. We have allowed our people, and even encouraged them, to fill our churches with cries of agony for those they loved, " Let this cup pass from them," and have allowed them to believe that it was prayer, provided they would add the great submission, " Thy will be done."

We have failed, in fact, to put first things first. The first thing, by far the first, that every Christian mother should learn to pray for her son, and every Christian wife for her husband, is that by him and through him, at whatever cost, God s will may be done. We must learn to leave the matter of life and death entirely in God s hands, and pray that in life or death our men may keep their manhood clean from every spot of cowardice or sin.

Especially must we teach our children this. The first prayer I want my son to learn to say for me is not " God keep daddy safe," but " God make daddy brave, and if he has hard things to do make him strong to do them." Life and death don t matter, Pat, my son ; right and wrong do. Daddy dead is daddy still, but daddy dishonoured before God is something awful, too bad for words. I suppose you d like to put in a bit about the safety too, old chap, and mother would. Well, put it in, but after wards, always afterwards, because it does not really matter near so much. Every man, woman, and child should be taught to put first things first in prayer, both in peace and war, and that I believe is where we have failed.

We have taught our people to use prayer too much as a means of comfort. Not in the original and heroic sense of uplifting, inspiring, strengthening, but in the more modern and baser sense of soothing sorrow, dulling pain, and drying tears. The comfort of the cushion, not the comfort of the Cross. Because we have failed in prayer to bear the Cross, we have also failed to win the crown.

From the soldier s point of view the condemnation of such prayers begins with the conviction, bought by bitter experience, that they do not work. Religion as an insurance policy against accident in the day of battle is discredited in the army. The men have lost what faith in it they ever had. Just as the rain descends upon the just and the unjust, so do the shells, and good and bad, praying and prayerless, are shattered into bits. It is terrible, but it is true ; as terrible and as true as life. The flying death that shrieks in a shell is as impartial as an avalanche or a volcano. It is as inevitable as the Cross. Though in their agony men cry to God if it be possible to let it pass, it will not pass if the laws by which it flies must bring it to your feet. As God did not quench the fires that burned the martyrs or close the lions mouths before they tore them limb from limb, so God does not turn aside the shell that flies shrieking out the call to martyrdom for me or for my son. Even as I pray now I may be blown to bits, as Christ, still praying, suffered on the Cross, and as His followers all down the ages have died the death with prayers upon their lips. Christ never promised to those who prayed immunity from suffering and death.

Well, then, what use is praying ? What answers do we win? We win the only answer worth having, the power to pass through danger and through death with a spirit still unbroken and a manhood still unstained.

In all these things we can be more than conquerors through Him Who loves us, because through prayer He can pour into us the gift of the splendid spirit. And it does not end there, for having poured it into us, He can, through our prayers for others, pour it through us into them. The splendid spirit can run through the men who really pray, like a stream of living fire, out into the world of men and women who need just that, and only that, for with that comes all that s best worth having in this world.

A shell is just an iron sin, like the nail that pierced His feet. It is just sin wrought into metal. Sin can be worked into any form. It is just a gift of God misused. Sin takes form and substance in a million ways : it pours forth in speech, it is painted in colours, it is built into bricks and mortar, it is carved into marble. Wherever a gift of God is misused sin takes form. It took the form of a wooden cross and crucified the Son of God; it takes the form of an iron shell and kills God s children by the score. War is just sin in a million forms in a million of God s gifts misused. God cannot deal with war in any other way than that by which He deals with sin. He cannot save us from war except by saving us from sin.

How does God deal with sin ? By what way does He conquer it ? By the way of the Cross, the way of love. He suffers for it ; He takes it upon Himself, and He calls on us to share His burden, to partake of His suffering. He makes an army of the Cross, an army of men and women who pledge themselves to fight with sin and gladly suffer in the fight, that by their strife and suffering the power of evil may be broken and the world redeemed.

Prayer is the means of communication by which the suffering and triumphant God meets His band of volunteers and pours His Spirit into them, and sends them out to fight, to suffer, and to conquer in the end.

Prayer will not turn away the shell from my body ; it will not change the flight of the bullet ; but it will ensure that neither shell nor bullet can touch me, the real me. Prayer cannot save me from sorrow, but it can draw the sting of sorrow by saving me from sin. And in the end, through prayer and the army of those that pray, God will reach down to the roots of war and tear them from the world. When at last through prayer the stream of the Spirit has flowed out to all, men will look upon their guns, their bombs, their gas cylinders as mad monstrosities, and will take the metal from the earth to mould and beat it, not into engines of death, but into means of beauty and of life.

Prayer, true prayer, will bring us victory. For victory comes at last to those who are willing to make the greatest venture of faith, and the supremest sacrifice. By prayer we can reach Berlin. But more than that, by prayer we can conquer war itself, and march at last into the New Jerusalem of God.

I mustn't curse this poor beggar. He's just gone under. He s lost the spirit. I was nearly as bad, for I had nearly lost it too. I must not curse him. I must pray for him. Probably I d better begin with a fag. Have a fag, lad ? I think it s dying down now. Yes, I've got a light. Christ the God the only God come down into his soul, and make him brave. Good God Almighty, what is that ? Are you there, sergeant ? Well, pull me out, will you. That chap s got it bad ; I ll go for stretcher-bearers. This lad s dead, and he never lit that fag. The cup could not pass. I hope he had braced himself to stand before the Christ... It must have been one of our own trench mortars, that.

The Hardest Part

VII: God and the Sacrament

ON the morning before the battle of June 7th, a large number of officers and men attended the Holy Communion. I noticed one corporal in particular whom I had never known to attend before. I remember thinking what a splendid young body his was as I said the words, " Preserve thy body and soul unto everlasting life" Three days later I buried his body, terribly mutilated, in a shell hole just behind the line.

I wonder why you came that morning, and did not come before. I wonder what you thought about this Service of the Broken Body and the Blood outpoured. I am sure you had the ordinary man s respect for it. You had a kind of feeling that it was a very special kind of service, not to be treated lightly or approached without thought. You probably felt that you were not and could not be good enough to come very often. It was to you a service for the very good for men who never swore, never drank too much, and never did a lot of things that you had done and might do again. You had the ordinary man s idea of goodness, the purely negative idea of not doing wrong, and so, because you knew that you often did wrong, and would probably keep on doing it, you did not come very often. The other day you were up against it ; you were faced with death. You were not really frightened, but you were dead serious, and you came. I wonder did you dimly hope that it might shield your body in the battle. Did you take the great words " Preserve thy body " literally ? Maybe you did. Superstition dies hard. I find it lingering in men s minds still, and in the minds of the most unlikely men, especially on religious subjects which they do not try to think about much. Was it thoughts of home that brought you ? Your mother would like to know that you had been. Your sweetheart always goes, and wanted you to go. Sentiment plays a large part in the ordinary man s religion. I've often known men come rather from love of mother or Mary, the girl, than from any conscious love of Christ. God bless them. I don t think Christ minds. Many a man finds God mainly through good women. It is a common road to Christ.

It was not a bad motive for coming, but it was not the best. The Sacrament evidently did not mean to you what it should mean, or you would have come more often. It would have been your food, and not your medicine. You are just typical of the rank and -file of the British. Your religion was made up of some superstition, more sentiment, and something else which yon did not understand ; but it was there, and was very like the real thing.

I wonder why we did not succeed, we who teach, in mating the Sacrament mean to you all that we believe it was intended to mean. I think it is quite evident that in a large number of cases we have not succeeded. I wonder why.

For some years now the teaching of all the Churches. Catholic and Nonconformist. has been increasingly strong on the Sacrament. We all agree now. far more than did, that it is the sum and centre of Christian worship, I have been much struck with that in talking to ministers of the English and Scottish Free Churches, the Roman Catholic Church has. of coarse, never abated her emphasis upon its absolute necessity, and her children are evidently much more devout in their attendance at it. and more regular. Yet neither we nor they have much ground for real satisfaction. In every Church there is a body of regular communicants surrounded by a larger body of occasional and irregular communicants, surrounded again by an enormous body of non- communicants who would still claim to be called Christians.

Perhaps that must always be so to some extent. It is the natural order in which the leaven would work in the lump. But I think we would all agree that the inner circle is far too small, and the two outer ones far too large. The inner circle is far too small, and too often, I fear, it is composed of the wrong sort of people. Too often, I am afraid, we find at our altars as regular communicants rather the comparatively little tempted than the actively and positively good. Many old and middle-aged women, some young girls, and a few very respectable men. I don t mean to despise or disparage them. Far from it. Probably England owes them more than she will ever know, but it does seem as though those who come to Christ s banquet are those who need it least. That is not good, is it?

We must not, on our peril, break down the barriers of instinctive reverence that surround the Altars and Communion Tables of our churches. We must make them stronger still. I think once more that we are agreed upon that. We must not make the great Food cheap, and yet we must not suffer those who really need it to starve their souls for lack of it.

I wonder if in our teaching about it we have not tended to make the Sacrament an end in itself rather than a means to an end, the great end of Christ-like life. It has seemed to the man in the street that we were trying to persuade him that regular and frequent attendance at this Service would of itself avail to save his soul, and secure him entry into heaven hereafter. We have failed, in fact, to connect the Sacrament with life. There is a great gulf fixed between the altar and the street, between the sacred and the secular. The man in the street feels instinctively that this is wrong. He feels that salvation depends upon character and not upon ceremonies. He has at last outgrown magic and mechanical religion. He regards it with the deepest suspicion. He may not be a good man himself, but he is quite sure that religious people ought to be good, positively and pre-eminently good. He will have nothing to do with religion which does not make character, and show itself a means to that end. He is sure that the Sacrament was made for man, and not man for the Sacrament. In this respect he is more Christian than the Church appears to be. Of course in theory we are just as much opposed to anything in the nature of magic and mechanical religion as he is, but in practice and in much of our teaching we sail very close to it. The Churches tend to become ends in themselves. We reckon our prosperity by the number of our communicants and the filling of our churches. The Churches war against the chapels, and in the struggle tend to lose sight of the end in view. The greater our reverence for the Sacrament, the stronger is the temptation to make it an end in itself, and insist upon it as a means not to fine life, but to salvation undefined.

Because we aim at filling our churches we empty them, and because we aim at crowding our Altars they are comparatively deserted. We have our small band of devotees, but the great tide of restless, vigorous life sweeps by our doors and finds outlet in a thousand other ways. We have been calling men to services when what they wanted was the call to service and to sacrifice. I think there is something in that, and other things have followed as a result of it. The Sacrament which was meant to be the centre of our Christian unity has become the source and centre of a most unchristian strife. The chorus of united praise that should have risen round our altars is broken into discords by our party cries. Our different ways of thinking about the Sacrament, and of interpreting our experience of It, have destroyed our unity and turned the Church into the warring Churches.

The great word Catholic has been degraded from its high estate and has become a party shibboleth. It has become associated with certain forms of ritual, and certain dogmatic expressions of Christian experience, and with a protest against all others. It has become the catchword of unchristian parties rather than the war-cry of the Christian Church. It has, in fact, completely changed its meaning. The real duty of a good Catholic is not to wear vestments and hate Nonconformists, but to love everybody and wear Christ. How utterly bewildering to the ordinary man all this division must be. Our interminable disputes on ritual questions and the method and meaning of the Real Presence, and the bitterness which they create what is he to make of them ? "I cannot make it out," he says; "aren t we all making for the same place ? " " Making for the same place " is the phrase which the bewildered man in the street uses to dismiss from his mind the problem of divided Churches. It is a vague loose phrase which the apostles of what is called definite religious teaching (generally, I m afraid, their own) are never tired of carping at, but it contains a truth which we would all do well to keep in mind. The truth is that our divisions are largely caused by the fact that we are not all " making for the same place," striving for one end, but each for our own end, which is really not an end at all, but a means disguised as one. There is a truth behind H. G. Wells bitter charge, " The Churches with their instinct of self-preservation at all costs." We have come to care more for our Churches and our parties than we care for our God. We have not kept ourselves from idols. Idolatry always divides and destroys where the worship of God would unite and create. The very centre of our idolatry is, to our shame, be it said, the Sacrament itself. That great gift more than others has tended to become an idol, as the Sabbath did to the Jews. The one thing that matters hi the Sacrament, as in everything else, is God. Of itself and in itself the going to the Sacrament could no more save us than going on a pilgrimage to Mecca. There is nothing magic or mechanical hi it. It is nothing unless it is a means of revealing God to human souls, whereby He comes to dwell in us and we in Hun. That is what It ought to be to all Christians, and what It is to those who have found Its secret. Why do so many neglect and forget It ? I fear it is because we have made the commandment of God of none effect through our traditions. We have either made attendance at the Sacrament an end itself to which our people came in blind obedience, trusting It would save their souls, or else we have obscured its simple truth by complex interpretations.

Broken bread and wine outpoured, quite simple things, what do they mean ? Is it not plain in the light of the Cross. The Sacrament is just the continual representing of the Cross. Coming to the Sacrament is coming to the Cross, and coming to the Cross is coming to God, the only God, Whose body is for ever broken and Whose blood is ever shed, until the task of creative redemption shall at last be all complete. The Cross is not really past, but present, ever present, and the Sacrament is the means of making its presence, or rather His presence, real to ourselves. It is a simple thing we do in remembrance of Him, out of love for Him ; and just be cause we do it out of love for Him, It makes Him real to us in a very special way.

It is all quite simple, but how complex we have made it, when we have tried to explain it at all, and have not been content to leave it as a mystery unexplained. Our dual vision of God has once more led us into endless complications. The Old Testament has again obscured the New. We have read into the Sacrament the Father on His throne accepting the sacrifice of the Son upon the Cross. We have made an absolute necessity of the Old Testament metaphor of sacrifice, and have clung to it as essential part of the truth. Our doctors have compiled a complicated theology which, amidst much wrangling and dispute, sets out to explain, not the Sacrament Itself, but the Old Testament metaphors used in the Epistle to the Hebrews and the Epistles of St. Paul, to express the inner meaning of the work and person of Christ. The very words in which these writers strove to express the inexpressible have been taken as sacred and essential, and of necessity the only vehicles for the truth in all ages. The splendid, passionate, grammarless rhetoric in which St. Paul splashed out, in his hurried but immortal letters, the truth that burned within him, has been treated as if it were the cold and carefully considered language of an academic professor. The idolatry of the Bible which gave rise to the idea that it was dictated word for word by the Almighty God has made the simplicity of the

The Hardest Part

Sacrament infinitely complex, because we have interpreted the Bible utterances about It according to the letter rather than the spirit. Sacramental controversy has become the delight of theologians and the despair of religious people.

Of course we could not expect the plain man to understand this infinitely complicated theology, so we said it was unnecessary for him to understand anything at all. He must come and ask no questions, and It would save His soul. We gave him a choice between stark mystery and a mass of complicated dogma. He is not satisfied, and does" not come. Can we wonder ? There is but one way to understand the Sacrament, the way in which the first Christians understood it. First they saw Him. They beheld His glory, glory as of the only begotten of the Father. In His suffering manhood they saw God, and learned to love and worship. Then, when His Body was taken away from them, they knew Him in the breaking of bread. The Sacrament was just Jesus Christ to them, and Jesus Christ was God. In Him it began, and in Him it ended. That is the truth, sublime in its simplicity the Sacrament is Christ, and Christ is God.

If we want our people to come to the Sacrament we must first of all give them the clear and shining vision of the Suffering God revealed in Jesus Christ, and then ask them to come to the service of the Broken Body and the Blood outpoured to meet Him, in order that by communion with Him they may be filled with His Spirit and inspired to suffer with Him, and so help to save and lift their comrades out of darkness into light. We must give them the vision first. The Sacrament was never meant to convert men to God. Conversion is the coming of the vision to the soul, and it must always come through men in whom Christ lives. Once the work of conversion is done, and a man has seen and loved God in Christ, then through the Sacrament the vision can be constantly renewed, and its power strengthened, until the man no longer lives, but God lives in Him through Christ. But the work of conversion comes first, and that is not the work of the Sacrament but of the prophet of God. No exaltation of the Sacrament can do away with the vital necessity of inspired men and women through whom the vision of the Suffering God can shine into the souls of men whose minds are still in the dark. The priest is not a substitute for the prophet. The prophet sows the seed, and the priest feeds the tender plant that springs up from it. Both are vitally necessary. Perhaps that is what our Nonconformist brethren have to teach us. They do realise more than we do that men need real prophets, real preachers. I hope when this business is over we shall each learn our lesson from the other, and go out together in the power of the Suffering God, speaking a simple Gospel with tongues of flame, and bearing a simple Sacrament with hands that tremble for the greatness of the precious thing they hold.

I think this mutilated body, and the thousand others like it, have taught me more of the meaning of the Sacrament than all the theology I ever read. In the days of peace the Broken Body and the Blood outpoured seemed to have so little to do with ordinary things in life. But here, broken bodies and pools of blood are the most ordinary things in life. So ghastly ordinary, always bodies, broken battered bodies, and always blood. Is it wrong to see in them His Body and His Blood God's Body, God's Blood ? They are His ; He is their Father, their Lover, and His Heart must bleed in them. Surely it is the simple truth of life and death. God suffers in man's suffering, and man, if he be man, suffers with God, and the world is saved by the suffering of God in man. The Cross, the Sacrament, the battlefield, there is the vision of God in them all God with outstretched, bleeding, pleading, patient hands calling for volunteers. These are they who answered the call, who have drunk God's cup, and been baptized with His Baptism, the dead who died for Right. These are men, and in them one sees the meaning of manhood.

To be a man means to be a thinking creature, filled with the spirit of suffering and creative love which made him.

The Sacrament is the means by which we become filled with that spirit. It is the heart, the blood centre, of the great army of men who, having seen and loved God in Christ, are resolved to fight for and suffer with Him unto death and beyond it. It is the appointed means and method of meeting God. We are ready to have our bodies broken and our blood shed in the great Christian warfare against wrong, and we come for the refreshing of our spirits that we may not shrink. That bread is the ration of a fearless, fiercely fighting army. That wine is the stirrup- cup of a band of knights who ride out to an endless war. Salvation is not a matter of the future, but of the present. Eternal life is here and now, and unless it is here and now, it cannot be hereafter. A famous soldier, speaking to troops on Whit-Sunday, said that he only wanted the soldier s virtues, and it would not matter to him if there were no Holy Spirit, so far had religion in his mind become divorced from life. There is but one Holy Spirit, the Spirit of Christ, and that is the most perfect soldier spirit in the world, the spirit of Divine heroism.

I wonder if you felt that dimly, Corporal. I wonder if you really came because you wanted to do your duty even to death, and wanted strength to do it. Did there flash into your mind the vision of heroic unselfishness, and did you love it, and come there to meet it ? If you did, then no theology can make you wiser and no dogma clear your vision. You may have been a Wesleyan, a Baptist, a Unitarian, but you ate the Body of the Lord and drank His precious Blood. You knew the truth. I wonder will your mother learn that truth through you. I wonder when she goes to bring her burden of sorrow before God, and kneels at the Altar rail, will she have strength to say :

The Hardest Part

> Dear Lord, I hold my hand to take
> Thy body broken here for me ;
>
> Accept the sacrifice I make,
>
> My body broken there for Thee.
>
> His was my body, borne of me,
> Borne of my bitter travail pain,
>
> And it lies broken on the field,
> Swept by the wind and rain.
>
> Surely a mother understands
>
> Thy thorn-crowned head,
> The mystery of Thy pierced hands,
>
> The broken bread.

Mothers and sons are learning the sternly simple truth of the Sacrament in a harder school than the Church, and from better masters than the priests. They know what it means, and we must learn from them and with them, or the nation will be more Christian than the Church. We must cut our selves adrift from the entanglement of needlessly complicated theology that has grown up around us in the course of the years, and must return to the stern simplicity of the truth.

Corporal, I wish you could come back, take up again your broken body, and tell us what you know. You would be wiser than the wisest of us. Perhaps we could not understand you if you did. Perhaps we know all we need to know. God suffers and God conquers, and calls on us to suffer and to conquer with Him. By this simple act, which Christ bade us perform, if it be done for love of Him, we can draw near to Him. He can speak to us and we to Him. He can fill us with

His Spirit. That is all we want to know, that is all we want to do do This in remembrance of Him Who is our God.

" O God of love and sorrow, relieve us of this weight of pride and prejudice which drags us down, and keeps us from Thee and from one another. We have degraded Thy Sacrament by pride of intellect and stubbornness of will, but by all these broken bodies, and by all this blood outpoured, bring our souls to Thy simplicity and the naked truth of Thee."

When this mad muddle is over and the days of peace return, there is a greater warfare still to wage. Still we must fight and still must suffer for the truth. God turn the Church from an ambulance into an army, and make it really militant on earth. Let us give up quarrelling with one another about the non-essentials, and leaving men large freedom about dogma and ritual, let us get to the real war with evil, and go in to win. Let us cease to dream of uniformity and strive for unity. One thing only matters. Do we love God ? Do we love the suffering God, and do we want to suffer with Him ? Do we find Him in the Sacrament ? Ritual does not matter ; the manner of the Presence does not matter ; the validity of orders does not really matter. They are not essentials. Nothing really matters but the love of God in Christ. That we must have. In all these non-essential matters let each Church be free to follow its custom and its bent, but let us endeavour to keep the unity of the spirit, the splendid spirit which is the only bond of peace.

Good-bye, Corporal. I ll write to mother for you. Thank you for dying for me, and teaching me so much. I will try to carry it out. The Church will, too. She is learning from the men that die. She will be more simple in the future. Christ is greater than the Church, and He can use her still, and through her revival He can save the world.

The Hardest Part

VIII: God and the Church

WANDERING in the Ypres salient about dawn on June 9th, 1917, I came across the body of a British soldier. He was still kneeling up on one knee in a shell-hole, grasping his rifle, with his face turned to wards the Green Line which two days before had cost our battalion many lives to win. His forehead was pierced with .a bullet which had evidently killed him instantly. His identity disc bore the name of Pte. Peter

---

Poor old Private Peter. Damn this war. I must get to work and bury him. Good thing I brought the shovel. I thought I'd find some one. Here s his pay book and a photo of his- wife and kids. Four of em. I must write to her. He couldn't have died better, anyhow. Evidently rose to advance and got it clean through the head. It s a fine fighting face ; no saint, but a fine man. A gentleman in his own way, as every British Tommy is. If faces go for much he was no saint. Heavy fighting jaw ; thick sensual lips ; deep lines round the eyes and mouth. They all tell the same tale. This was man Peter fine man, Peter, but no Saint Peter. I should not think he was a pillar of the Church. Not the sort of stuff we build them of. Yet, I don't know.

    I wonder what sort of a man Saint Peter was before he met Christ. He could curse and swear ; we know that. He evidently went back to the old days on the lake of Galilee when that maidservant tripped him up. He was married, and knew a man s passion. He had a nickname, too ; that always means a lot. Christ called him " Rocky," as soon as He saw him almost. It must have been a joke on his appearance. He wasn't much like a rock really. You never knew quite where you had him ; he was swearing fidelity one minute, and denying it the next. Now ready to die for Christ in the garden, a sword in his hand and battle in his eyes ; now

The Hardest Part

creeping away into a corner, afraid of jeers and jokes and the chaff of a silly girl. Half a hero, half a sheep. He brings joy to the eyes of Jesus by a splendid confession of faith, and the next moment makes those same eyes flash fire by crass misunderstanding. Blessed art Thou Simon, Bar-Jonah . . . Get thee behind me, Satan. Heaven and hell, God and the devil, rolled in one and for ever at war. That was Saint Peter. That was Private Peter too. You can see the traces of the struggle written deep into his face.

Why shouldn't Private Peter be a stone in the foundation of the Church ? Why did Christ choose Saint Peter for one ? Of course the great promise was partly a joke. I am sure it was said with a smile. The play upon the name is full of that splendid humour which is made up of love and faith in human greatness and sorrow for its faults. It was a joke, but it was more. Why did He choose Peter ? Was it because he was an exceptional man ? Was he the greatest and the strongest of that little band ? I doubt it. There's not much sign of it that I can see. One can t help loving Saint Peter ; he was so human, so weak, so strong, so great, and so small. He was just a splendid specimen of the average man, the incarnate paradox of God. That s why he was chosen, I believe. Not because he was exceptional, but because he was good average. Found an empire on a strong man s strength, and it will die when the strong man dies ; found an empire on a weak man s faith, and it will last for ever.

The secret of victory lies in the spirit of the rank and file. The Kingdom of God is within you. Christ knew that ; He was the leader of men. Peter was a splendid specimen of the rank and file, and when he grasped the truth and sprang to it, Christ cheered, because He knew the job was done. Christ in the soul of the average man is the rock foundation of the Church. St. John and St. Paul were exceptional men. They build the towers and the turrets of the Church, but the foundation is laid in the heart of St. Peter, the private in the Army of the Cross. That is why the history of the Church is so like the history of an ordinary man. It is full of splendid deeds and sordid crimes; full of glorious aspirations and silly sinful futile failures. An infallible Church is as hard to conceive as an infallible man. It simply couldn't happen.

Look at the life of the average man with the eyes of love, and you can see God. You cannot see God Almighty Whose will works out perfection without a struggle or a hitch. You cannot see that even in the saint. But in the saint and in the average man you can see God in an agony of creative effort, God crucified, but conquering, Christ.

Look at the history of the Christian Church, and you see the same vision. The Church is the broken, battered, bleeding, but deathless body of the suffering God revealed in Christ. How often have men cried out that the Church was dead, that the body was putrified, corrupt in every part, stinking of avarice and deceit, eaten up by the worms of political intrigue, torn by factious pride and petty personal ambition, a useless carcase, only fit for burial in the grave of a disreputable past. How often has the cry seemed to be justified by facts. Yet the Church does not die, it turns in its death-sleep like its Master in the tomb, and rises again, still bearing in its hands and feet the signs of suffering, but alive with a deathless life. Church history makes the Christian now bow his head in shame, now lift it up in pride ; but once he sees its story not as the history of a Society or even of the Society, but as the history of his God at war with evil, the very shame that stains its annals makes him love it all the more. The Church is a failure. Men keep shouting that out. Of course it is. All great things are failures; only little things succeed. The Church fails as God fails, as Christ failed upon the Cross, and it succeeds with His success, the success of the Crucified. When most the Church is beaten, when her standards are mocked, despised, and trampled under foot, when she is harassed most by spies and traitors from within and enemies without, then is her appeal for loyalty most strong and her real power appears.

Her real power appears, and shows itself to be the appeal of the suffering God revealed in Christ to the heart of the average man.

But this vision of God is obscured by that other vision which we set up beside it, the vision of the regnant God upon a throne, calm, serene, and passionless, ruling the world with a wave of the hand. How can men see that God in the Church? How can you expect men to look at the wounded, crippled, crucified Church as she is at present, and as she has been in the past, torn by a thousand factions, cut into a thousand silly sects, bound hand and foot and hanging helpless on the cross of a world wide war, with her voice drowned by the roar of guns and the groans of dying men how can they look at her and see God Almighty ? The ordinary man has this vision of the Almighty God and looks for it in the Church. Can you wonder that he is at once puzzled and disappointed ? Is it not St. Peter over again ? He had it of course. He got it from the Old Testament ; that was why he was puzzled to death when Christ told him that the Son of God must be mocked and spit on, tortured and killed. He could not understand the suffering God ; he shrank from that terrible truth. " This be far from Thee, Lord, " he cried, and Christ recognised the enemy, and hissed out " Satan " at him. It was the ancient enemy. Men will make God an earthly king. The natural man cannot see the King upon the Cross. Peter found that the hardest of all lessons to learn, and men have shared his feelings ever since. St. Peter did learn it. He learnt it through tears, and terror, and fires of shame that were not quenched. That made him the rock indeed at last.

I don t think Private Peter learnt it. I think he died without seeing it died without seeing it after two thousand years of Christ. Why? Whose fault was it? Was it his own ? Well, partly for sure. I know men too well to be humbugged by the sickly sentimental " John Bull " idea of the perfect hero touch. I think he failed to be a pillar of the Church partly because he was a pillar of the " Pig and Whistle." But was it all his fault? I don t think so. It was partly my fault, and the fault of those like me whom Christ sent out to teach him. We did not teach him right. We did not give him the true vision of God ; we had not got it ourselves. We, too, feared to face the facts, and to look upon the face of the suffering God. We sentimentalised the Cross, the greatest fact of all. We dared to glorify Christ with our earthly glory, which is a heavenly shame. We were Satan to a million Peters, because we thought the thoughts of earth and failed to speak the speech of heaven.

Private Peter would have told you that he believed in a Supreme Being. This Being ordered the details of men s lives and arranged the hour of their deaths. He managed everything, and everything that happened was His will. That was the faith that Peter, on being taxed with it, would probably have professed. But it did not interest him or make any difference to him. In truth he did not really believe it in any living sense. It was not his own faith ; it was borrowed. Dimly, I believe, he felt that it was absurd in the face of facts. This Supreme Being (which is the plain man s name for " The Unknown God ") was a puzzle which he could not solve. He was there, of course, but He could neither know nor love Him, His ways of working were so weird. He looked at the mangled body of a pal, muttered " I dunno," lit his fag, took up his rifle, and went out to die, because it was up to him and probably died without the vision of God.

That s a pretty ghastly thought. Peter, old chap, I m sorry. I m awful sorry, it was my fault. I should have told you more. We chaps who wear our collars wrong way round as a queer kind of sign that we preach Christ, we should have reached you, and we didn't. We re sorry, and it makes us sick. We re sorry, not only because we love you, but because we love the Church. It s a bad thing when the Church fails to produce great saints, but it is a worse thing when she fails to find the heart of the average man. That she should have no towers or turrets to catch the dawn light of the higher truth is

The Hardest Part

a bad thing, but that she should be shaky in her foundations is a worse one, and her foundations ought to be in your heart and in the heart of those like you.

That's our trouble, Peter, my son ; that s our trouble. We are missing the average man. Here I am, digging your grave ; it s all I can do, but I wish I could have done more. I ll have to drag you to it, old chap; it s beastly, but I must. I can t lift you up. The dead weigh heavy on the hand, and on the heart. Poor woman, and poor kiddies! When I ve finished filling in I ll get a couple of sticks and put up a bit of a cross for you. I don t think you knew what it meant in life, but you have probably found out through death. There, that s finished.

Now for the cross. Lord, I hope they re not going to start shelling. I m going to put this cross up, anyhow. Here are two bits of wood ; I've got some string some where, I know. That s the way. The Tree. The Cross of Christ. You did not know it, but you died for the cause of Christ, in defence of that civilisation which He has slowly and painfully built up in the western world. Its not much of a cross, I m afraid, but it is more like His, and so more really beautiful, than the gold and jewelled ornaments that glitter on our altars at home. This rough cross, and the million others like it, will be a challenge to the world and to the Church of Christ, calling them out to war for Him. I ll do my best, Peter ; I swear by this cross I will. I ll go and tell the other Peters about the suffering God, and how He is crucified afresh every day, and how He needs men like you to come out and share His sorrow and help to save the world. Perhaps they won t fight any better when they know ; I don t see how they could; but they will know that they are suffering with God, and will feel that He is near. That s a great thing. I know it is. I ve felt it. Men like you must worship Him when they see Him; He would appeal to all that s best in you. Only, you must get the vision. It won t be done by preaching half so much as living, and yet there must be both. Peter, my lad, living is a durned difficult business, much harder than dying. I think I could die for Christ, but living for Him is a struggle. But I will try to live as the servant of the gallant God Who suffers always and is never overcome. I ve got to do some of the preaching too. I m not fit to preach; but who is? That s the awful business. Preaching is so much mixed up with living. How can one put the vision into words ?

There is so much barbed wire entanglement to get through before I can hope to get the message to the men I want to reach. The Church herself has done a lot of wiring in her war of the ages, and now she must tear it down. At the beginning the Church beat the world by suffering ; later, the world beat the Church by compromise. The Church borrowed the world s weapons and the world s ideals. She took the sword, and very nearly perished by it. The glory of the world s great kings obscured the glory of the Christ. Men would have no king but Caesar, and the Church, because she feared the world, was feign to Csesarise the Christ. The vision of God which she presented to the world grew dim and distorted. The ordinary man was puzzled. The Almighty Caesar God seated on His throne alternated with the suffering figure on the Cross, and the Peters of the world did not know which was the true God. Later on, the worship of the Bible made it worse. The partial truth of the Old Testament obscured the final truth of the New, because Peter was taught to think of them as equally true. The Bible was an idol, and obscured the truth of Christ which it was written to reveal. The figure of Christ Himself was distorted, and His life on earth misinterpreted in order to reconcile the two visions of God. The glorious rebellion of Christ against evil, the fierce and lifelong war which found its culmination on the Cross, has been distorted into passive submission to the mysterious, and apparently immoral, will of the unknown Caesar God Who planned that men should torture, mock, and crucify the Christ. The foulest, filthiest crime in the world s history has been held up as God s plan, God s chosen method of saving the world, the finest fruit of His absolute omnipotence. Led by this false vision the Church played the world's game. Christianity, which was meant to turn the world upside down, became a means of keeping it wrong way up. Great Christians ceased to be rebels and became policemen constables of Almighty God.

Submission to the world order became a Christian virtue, and took the place of that tremendous Christian aspiration which should have smashed the world order into pieces. The Church fought against demands for social justice, and the abolition of social evils. She became other-worldly in the wrong way, and taught men the lesson of indifference not only to sorrow, but to injustice, oppression, and cruelty. Her rulers allied themselves with the strong against the weak, and devoted their energies to keeping the people quiet. They taught contentment as the chiefest of all virtues. Blessed are they that neither hunger nor thirst after righteousness, for they shall be called respectable. Blessed are the poor in pocket, for they shall be patronised by the rich. Blessed are they who do not mourn for the wrong in the world, for they shall need no comfort. Blessed are they that expect nothing, for they shall not be disappointed. Christianity became static instead of dynamic, because it taught men to worship a passive and submissive Christ, bowing to the will of an incomprehensible God.

Neither the submissive Christ nor the tyrant God has any appeal to what is best in Peter the average man ; they leave him cold. The sporting instinct, the love of fair play, the hatred of injustice, the fine combative instinct, which make up the character of Peter, have remained un-touched by this staggering, broken-spirited, submissive figure on the Cross, Who, in the words of a popular mission hymn, " died of a broken heart," and these same splendid instincts have been actually raised to bitter antagonism by vision of the tyrant God.

So Peter has left the Church, and found what his soul needed in his union, his club, his cause the cause of the downtrodden and oppressed. This has taken place, and is taking place, not only in England, but in every country in the world. Everywhere the followers of Christ are found outside the Church. The Church of Christ has ceased in these days to be the pillar of cloud and fire which leads the pilgrim Peter along the way of social righteousness, and has become a weak and inefficient ambulance brigade which picks up the wreck and ruin of a cruel and mechanical civilisation. That s all I am, Peter, an informal and incompetent undertaker, with tears in my eyes and sorrow in my heart, and I m very like the Church I represent. We dig mens graves when we ought to save their souls, because we have, and give to others, a distorted vision of God.

But that is not the whole truth, Peter. There is another side. Christ has used the Church, and spoken through her in spite of her stupidity and sin. Some of your comrades found the truth in her, and loved her. To some she brought the strength to suffer and to fight for right. Crippled, tortured, crucified as she is, she has the root of the matter in her. Christ still uses her. And believe me, Peter, she is going to do better. She knows her weakness, and that means much ; she knows she has betrayed her Lord, but at any rate in this war she has gone out to weep bitterly.

And let me whisper this, lad: she loves you, she really loves you, she is not the Church of a class any longer at heart. She means to reform. She is not going to read your comrades impossible stories out of the Old Testament on Sundays. She is going to reform her money matters, which have been a scandal. The bishops are very uncomfortable in their palaces. The Prayer Book is going to be revised. The parson is going to stop being God Almighty in a little narrow world and become brother-man. Please, Peter, poor old dead Peter, the man with his collar wrong way round is very sorry, and is going to do better, and show your comrades Christ, the suffering, conquering Christ, Who calls us out to the glorious war with evil that is not fought with guns calls us to enlist in the ever-fighting army of the suffering God.

There, that will do. It's a poor show of a cross, but you know what is meant. I hope old Boche won t knock it down before we get a stronger one. " O Christ my God, my only God, Eternal Spirit of strong love, give unto Thy Church a fuller measure of Thy Spirit, that for the sake of such as these she may sanctify herself."

Good-bye, Peter, old chap ; I ll write to the missus, and I'm going to follow Christ.

IX: God and the Life Eternal

ON the last Sunday in June 1917 the Advanced Dressing Station in which I was working was blown in, and every one in it killed except the doctor, two stretcher cases, an R.A.M.C. sergeant, and myself. Among those killed was Roy Fergusson, my servant, a splendid lad of nineteen years, with whom I was great friends. He went out after the first shell had broken the end off the station to guide some walking wounded to a place of safety and was killed instantly. I found him leaning against a heap of sandbags, his head buried in his hands, and a great hole in his back.

Poor old Roy. I thought I had saved his life when I sent him on that job. There seemed a decent chance of getting through, and it looked a dead certainty that we should all be killed within a few minutes. There must have been a chance. All the walking wounded apparently got through, and he alone was killed. He probably warned them and took it himself. It would be like him. He looks as if he were saying his prayers. I must get the body carried across to the cemetery near Railway Dug outs, and bury it at once. It will probably be unburied again before the morning if they start shelling again. That cemetery is an awful sight, with half its dead unburied ; but it is the only place. I must give the body Christian burial somewhere, even if it is blown up again. His mother will surely want to know where he rests. Mothers always want to know that first. I wonder why. Do they think that this same broken body will break the earth above its grave and rise again to become once more the temple of the spirit that has passed on ? Do they think that it matters in the resurrection where the body lies, or is it just a natural longing, an echo of Mary's exceeding bitter cry beside the empty tomb, " They have taken away my Lord, and I know not where they have laid Him."

The Hardest Part

The first Easter Day should have hushed that cry for ever and turned its sorrow into joy, but it has not done so for many who love and follow Christ. Still men and women seem to seek the living midst the dead, and to think of their dead as lying in their graves. They always want to know where the dead are buried. It may be natural sentiment, or it may be false religion. Anyway, that s not my business now. Sentiment or religion, the desire is there, and I must do my best to satisfy it. A Padre out here has got to be an amateur undertaker. So ghastly amateur, that is the worst of it. We cannot hope to bury half the dead. Many a mother s aching heart must go uncomforted because we know not where we have laid him. No one knows. Some are not buried, because there is nothing to bury but scraps of flesh and clothing. Some are buried, and then blown to pieces out of their graves. There is an enormous crater in the middle of the cemetery, and the bodies are not ; that s all that can be said. But where Christian burial can be given, it must be given, if only for pity s sake.

I say, you chaps, this lad was my servant. Could you help me across with him to the cemetery. You ll have to lift him very carefully, he s so badly shattered. That s the way. Now we ll carry him across and have the service while the lull is on. There is a grave ready. Would you mind staying while I say the service over him ?

No, you need not stay to fill in, boys. I ll do that. Thank ye very much. It only saddens them, and what s the use ? I wonder why Christian men and women still think of their dead as lying in their graves. I suppose the Church is partly responsible. The burial service, with all its wonderful beauty, is very hard to understand. It is difficult to gather from it what the Church does believe about the future of the body it lays in the grave. It consigns it to the earth as ashes to ashes and dust to dust, and then speaks of the resurrection in which Christ shall change our poor bodies that they may be like unto His glorious body. It seems to mean that this same body will some day break the earth that covers it, and rise to life again. Our hymns contain the same idea :

> For a while the tired body
> Lies with feet toward the morn.
> Till that last and greatest Easter
> Day be born.

And that astounding verse :

> Days and moments quickly flying,
> Blend the living with the dead ;
> Soon will you and I be lying
> Each within his narrow bed.

It is poor poetry, and I cannot help feeling that it contains really false teaching. Neither you nor I nor any one else will ever lie in any narrow bed. Our bodies will for a time, and will then rot, and, decomposing, will become part of the earth. It is, I take it, dead certain that this sad wilderness of war will one day be clothed with a festive robe of living green, decked with daisies, and that the life that weaves this robe will spring from the bodies of our British dead. They will give life to the dying seed, and produce the fields of golden grain from which the new France will gain its strength. This will be the resurrection of these bodies buried here.

We cannot now believe that there will ever come a time when these same bodies will burst their graves and rise from broken trenches and from shell holes, living men. If men ever believed it, we cannot believe it now. In face of facts out here the attempt to believe it can only lead to bewilderment. What a picture it would be! when the dead who followed Napoleon stand up with those who followed

Joffre; when the French who cursed the British with their last breath stand up with these brave Poilus who blessed us as they died the last roll-call when all shall answer, Present, and friend stand side by side with foe. What a picture for a poet or a painter! but it is only an imaginary picture; nothing more. It could never be a fact. I don t suppose that any one who thinks and faces facts believes it now, yet, on the surface at any rate, much of our Church teaching seems to contemplate it. The creed in the Baptism Service contains " The resurrection of the flesh." It is a great question which St. Paul s objector asks, and is called a fool for asking, " How are the dead raised up, and with what body do they come ? " St. Paul s answer is by no means clear. It is glorious in its conviction that the spirits of those who die in Christ survive death, and are clothed by God with a body; but as to the nature of that body and its connection with the flesh that is buried, it is distinctly vague.

 The first part of the answer is quite intelligible and satisfactory. The resurrection body is related to the fleshly body as a flower to its seed, i.e. it is the same body only in the sense that it is the clothing of the same life. In appearance and in actual composition, I suppose it is entirely different. That is quite clear and helpful. He goes farther, and definitely states that the two bodies must of necessity be different. " Flesh and blood cannot inherit the Kingdom of God ; neither doth corruption inherit incorruption." That is exactly what we feel in the present day. Then a sense of difficulty seems to come over his mind, and he cries, " Behold I show you a mystery," and there breaks upon us once again some thing very like the gloriously impossible picture. There is the blare of the trumpet, the whole air quivers with expectation, the graves slowly yawn, and the dead are raised all the countless millions who have stood on earth and looked upon the sun. It is a wonderful passage, and has gripped the imagination of men for nearly two thousand years. But what does it mean ? It seems to contradict the other more reasonable statement.

Corruption puts on incorruption, and mortal puts on immortality, and the dead are raised incorruptible. What does it mean ? Is it poetry or prose ? Is it emotional allegory or literal statement of fact?

I feel sure it is the usual outburst of splendid spiritual emotion which sooner or later always bursts through the bounds of the Pauline arguments, and shattering all syllogisms, breaks into a song of certainty which soars above reason into fields of faith. These outbursts are what make the Pauline Epistles immortal, and men will thrill to their music when the arguments of Paul the learned Pharisee leave them unconvinced and cold.

St. Paul's answer seems to mean that there are more things in heaven and earth than are dreamed of in the very narrow philosophy of the man who refuses to believe in the resurrection because of the difficulty of the visible decomposition of the flesh. "Leave it to God," he says in effect ; " leave it to God Who raised up Christ." Who raised up Christ that is the one root -fact which inspires this chapter. Christ was dead and is alive again. That is the one vivid certainty which shatters all doubts for St. Paul. He has no real theory of the resurrection body to give us, and no real answer to the question " How are the dead raised up, and with what body do they come ? " He has only a vivid intuitive conviction that, as Christ conquered death and rose again, so the man who lives hi Christ and in whom Christ lives can conquer death, and live on hereafter with a full embodied life, and not in any shadowy kind of existence which the heathen as a rule believed to be the state of the dead.

That seems to be the real point of the great funeral chapter. It all turns and hinges on the fact of Easter Day.

There is in all the letters of St. Paul a continual confusion between physical and spiritual death, and it is very hard at times to tell which he means. I suppose the reason of that confusion is that, to him, there is only one kind of death worth bothering about, and that is spiritual death, which is the climax and final result of sin. Physical death was only death to him when it was the material expression of this spiritual death. That, I think, is the great truth. I have seen physical death which was real death, the last and bitterest enemy of man. That death was defeat, defeat and disaster: a broken, peevish, sordid spirit reluctantly hounded out of a body which it had weakened by disease and defiled by misuse. That is real death, the saddest and most repulsive thing on earth. From such a death may God deliver me and all I love. But that death and this boy's splendid exit are two quite different things. There is something triumphant about this. It has no connection with disease or decay. A young spirit quivering with life and energy has, in an act of supreme sacrifice, thrown off its earthly raiment and leaped glad and naked into another world to receive the best robe of sonship from the Father God. It is true there is no sting in this, because there is no sin. This is not defeat, but victory through Jesus Christ our Lord.

Roy was a fine Christian. What about men who aren't? There are many men who die fine deaths who have no faith, or at least no conscious faith, in God or Christ as Son of God. How about them? Well, God is greater than the Churches. He is the source, and the only source, of all fine life of the spirit. If a man dies for duty's sake a death which is for his spirit not defeat but victory, he dies in Christ. That is how it looks to me. Christ is the Lord of all good life. He is the only source of the splendid life of the spirit which turns defeat in death to victory. This gift of the "life eternal" is indeed poured out upon men through the Church and the appointed means of grace, but we cannot confine God to His covenants. The river of eternal life breaks through a thousand channels and finds the soul of man.

I don't mean by that to subscribe to the rather sentimental idea that every man who dies in battle attains automatically to the perfection of eternal life. God only knows how each man dies. There may be real death on a battle-field as well as in a sick-room.

Two bodies may lie side by side upon the same battle-field, both shattered by the same shell, and their two spirits may stand in the other world in utterly different states, one weak and wounded, defiled and defeated by sin, and the other strong and radiant, having conquered death in the spirit. It is not the act of death which counts, but the spirit of it. That seems to be St. Paul s idea, and I believe it is profoundly true.

A critic might suggest that it was all emotional assumption, without any solid basis of fact. It is not really that. It is based upon the fact of Christ and the revelation of God that fact contains. It is true that the vivid certainty which makes the fact of Christ for Christians the crowning fact of life, is the direct result of spiritual communion with God in Christ, and that this communion is an act, not of the intellect, but of the spiritual faculty. Nevertheless, the intellect plays its proper part in the mind of St. Paul and of other thinking Christians. The intellect cannot give certainty in anything except purely abstract sciences like mathematics ; its normal function is to provide probability as a basis of intuitive certainty, and to follow faith, which is its lodestar, along the paths of mystery which lead to real truth.

It plays this proper part both for St. Paul and for us in our faith concerning eternal life. St. Paul believed that Christ conquered death and rose again on historical evidence which was sufficient to satisfy his intellect. He goes through this evidence at the beginning of the chapter, recounting the appearances of Christ to trustworthy witnesses after death. This evidence, combined with certain facts which he himself had observed the sublime hero ism of St. Stephen and the calm conviction of many Christian men and women whom he himself had put to death for Christ s sake struck his mind, and, thinking on it, prepared the way for the vivid spiritual vision of the risen Christ which was the basis of his whole Christian life. The intellect provided the living and disturbing probability as a basis for the glorious intuitive certainty which was his inspiration.

That is always the way with thinking Christians. For us to-day there is the disturbing probability of the resurrection which rests on facts. There is for us a larger fact of Christ, which in honesty we ought to face. There is not merely the story of His death and resurrection as told in the Gospels, which, isolated and of itself, would not perhaps be convincing, but there is the fact of what Christ has done. There is the history of Western civilisation, with the risen Christ at its core and centre. Men say that this civilisation has broken down and been destroyed, but that is shallow talking. It never was so strong as it is to day in the hearts of the Allied nations ; it is so strong that men by millions prefer death to life without it. Never were sane men so certain of the truth of Christ as they are when they see it against the background of this insanity of barbarism.

European history, and indeed the history of the world, is to me an insoluble riddle apart from the resurrection of Christ. When one tries to picture the death of Christ upon the Cross as the end of His story, one is left staring at history in a state of utter bewilderment, as one would stare at an effect which appeared without a cause. Thus we have our basis of intellectual probability, but it is only a basis. The mere intellectual assent to the fact of the risen Christ could not of itself inspire a man with certainty and a sense of victory over death. That certainty can only be provided by spiritual communion with God through Christ, and that communion is an act, not of the intellect, but of intuition of faith. Of course this business of separation between intellect and intuition is, as usual, a process of convenient but impossible abstraction, but it is almost necessary for thought. Bergson taught me much. What a comic combination Bergson and Boche bombardments make ! It comes back to this : The only source of a living certainty and a sense of victory over death is a vision of God. Where there is no open vision, the people perish, and faith in the life thereafter grows dim ; where the vision of God is unclouded, faith rises supreme and triumphant over death. Once more we find it true. It is God that matters. God alone can give the victory over death. Everything depends upon a man s vision of God.

But then, in battle men go mad; they have no vision of anything : they see red. Every man who dies in a bayonet charge dies mad what about them ? If madness means anything it means that a man s actions have no moral or spiritual significance whatever, but are just mechanical results of his surroundings. In their case the act of death can have no spiritual meaning. Quite so ; but the spiritual act took place before the madness. There is a Gethsemane before every Calvary, and there the cup is either taken or refused. The soldier can say with St. Paul, " I die daily " ; and as he faces the daily death of ever- present danger, so he will face the real shadow when it comes.

As a matter of fact, almost every man who dies in battle dies under a natural ansesthetic of some sort. If nature had not a supply of anaesthetics the finest battalions would turn and run. Flesh and blood could not stand it unless our sensibilities were deadened, but the nature of the anaesthetic is largely determined by a man s character and convictions. It may be the madness of excitement, or the dullness of despair, or the numbness of extreme terror, or it may be the splendid recklessness of sacrifice based upon entire devotion to duty and to God ; but in every case it is a man s daily life that determines the spirit of his death, and his vision of God that determines his daily life.

There may be apparently sudden conversions on the battle-field as there are on death-beds, but in both cases they are probably the result of a change that has been gradually coming over a man s spirit. Real conquest over death can only be obtained by real redemption from sin.

The measure of a man s victory over death is the measure of his victory over sin. No amount of purely intellectual conviction of immortality could or would accomplish a man s redemption from death. " If they believe not Moses and the prophets, neither will they believe though one rose from the dead." The living hope of life eternal must be founded on faith in God. Faithless hope is as sad and as weak as despair. That is what Watts would teach us in his picture of Hope. He depicts the rationalistic nineteenth century seated on the summit of the world, and commanding a view of the whole universe from those dizzy heights of material know ledge which progressive science has enabled her to climb. All her knowledge cannot comfort her soul. She cannot bear to look upon the picture it opens out to her, and so she blinds her eyes and strains her ears to the one unbroken string from which music can be wrung, the string of hope. " If in this life we have only hope in Christ, we are of all men most miserable." That is the correct translation of that text, and it is a profound truth. Positive and powerful hope can only spring from faith and in communion with the suffering, but deathless and conquering, God Who reached the soul of St. Paul with a cry of splendid agony, " I am Jesus Whom thou persecutest." We need such positive hope to-day as we never needed it before. We must have it if we are to rise as a nation from our present sorrow, having won from it new life and power. We are now bearing our burden very largely on the false stimulant of drugs the common drugs of drink, vice, pleasure- seeking, self-deception, and wilful blindness to the facts. The nation too often turns for refuge from the hideous facts of war, not to its higher but to its lower self, and tries to drown its sorrows in the waters of Lethe. Our aim is to forget, because we dare not remember. God forbid that I should condemn wholesale the spirit of my people, or fail to appreciate their splendid heroism I too have longed to forget, craved for an anaesthetic, and have taken them in hours of weakness but I believe there is real danger lest we fail to reap the fruits of this purgatory of pain because we seek not to remember but to forget, and, unlike Christ, Who turned His head away and refused the myrrh and wine, drink deep and eagerly of any drug that deadens pain.

The nation needs this hope now, and it will need it always. Nations cannot keep their heads on earth unless their hearts are fixed in heaven. They inevitably suffer from the madness of materialism unless they have the living hope of life eternal which puts our earthly life into its true perspective as something, not indeed un important, but certainly not all important, or even of the first importance. The comparative failure in modern times of real hope of life eternal is largely responsible for the insanity of dreary materialism which has issued in a temporary throw-back into barbarism and the outbreak of this cursed conflict.

The only way in which this hope can be quickened and revived among men is by giving them an open vision of God, a vision which can be seen by men without a wilful refusal on their part to face in their fullness the darker facts of life. Everything which obscures the vision of God weakens faith in life eternal. It is because the Church persists in presenting to men to-day a vision of God which the facts of life as men know them now render impossibly obscure and incredible, that she is failing to satisfy their hunger for this living hope. They are turning away from her in bitterness and disappointment, because she has no food to offer which will appease the hunger of their hearts. And because they must have something, they are seeking for comfort in Spiritualism and the discoveries of those engaged in psychical research.

Psychical research is a perfectly legitimate study and was bound to be taken up by man. The evidence for the survival of the human personality after death accumulated by men like F. W. H. Myers and Sir Oliver Lodge is legitimate evidence, and contains its measure of comfort for the troubled intellect. It can, however, never take the place of the lively hope which comes of faith in and communion with God I am grateful for all such evidence ; it helps satisfy my intellect when it is inclined to doubt, because it provides new facts which are very difficult, if not impossible, to account for on a materialistic basis ; but of and in itself it would not satisfy the needs of my nature in regard to immortality. It is not a source of spiritual vital energy, and has no power to inspire me with a sense of victory over death and give me the lively hope, not merely of existence, but of fuller and more splendid life beyond the grave. What we need is moral and spiritual energy, and this is what these studies cannot supply ; indeed, the study of psychic phenomena, as experience shows, is dangerous for any but healthy and well-balanced minds, and would be a disastrous substitute for ethical religion.

Such evidence as it affords does not in any way contradict the faith of Christians. Christ told us practically nothing about the conditions of the life hereafter, beyond the plain fact that our fate there depended upon the use we made of our powers here. The reason of this reticence I believe was that, if He had told us, we could not have under stood, having no faculties for such under
standing. This appears to be confirmed by the meagreness of the communications which the dead are able to make with us, and the fact that their ability to communicate be comes less by lapse of time. There are no words and no method of speech by which we can be made to understand the conditions of life in the other world. The evidence seems to support the idea of a kind of purgatorial progress after death. This has always been the Christian teaching. The abolition of purgatory was one of the temporary absurdities due to the reaction of the Reformation against abuses. The ideas of progress and purification are essential to our thought about the hereafter. Eternal life, as St. John says, is progressive knowledge of the only true God, and Jesus Christ Whom He has sent.

The turning to Spiritualism is sad, because it will ultimately fail to satisfy the real needs of man. At best it can give only hope, hope that is based not on faith, but on doubt and despair, and that does but make us the more miserable. We come back to the bed-rock truth. The sting of death is sin, and real redemption from death is just redemption from sin. God alone can go to the root of the trouble and conquer death by pouring life into the soul. To the man who has learned the secret of the love of God in Christ, death has only the uncertainty of a glorious adventure. He does not know the way by which he will climb after death, and he neither expects nor desires to know it. It is enough for him that he knows and trusts his guide. He will in this life be " steadfast, unmovable, always abounding in the work of the Lord," because he knows through Christ that his labour is not vain in the Lord." I am sure we have obscured the vision of God because we feared to face the facts of life. We have been ashamed of the Cross and have shrunk from the suffering God. This is what men need, the love of the suffering God of God in Christ ; then, and only then, all things are theirs the world, and life and death and things present and things to come ; all things are theirs, for they are Christ s and Christ is God's.

> Bed with His blood, the better day is dawning ;
> Pierced by His pain the storm clouds roll apart ;
> Rings o er the earth the message of the morning,
> Still on the Cross the Saviour bares His heart.
>
> Passionately fierce the voice of God is pleading,
> Pleading with men to arm them for the fight ;
> See how those hands, majestically bleeding,
> Call us to rout the armies of the night.
>
> Not to the work of sordid selfish saving
> Of our own souls to dwell with Him on high ;
> But to the soldier s splendid selfless braving,
> Eager to fight for righteousness and die.
>
> Peace does not mean the end of all our striving,
> Joy does not mean the drying of our tears ;

Peace is the power that comes to souls arriving
Up to the light where God Himself appears.

Joy is the wine that God is ever pouring
Into the hearts of those who strive with Him,
Lighning their eyes to vision and adoring,
Strengthning their arms to warfare glad and grim.

Bread of Thy Body give me for my fighting,
Give me to drink Thy Sacred Blood for wine ;
While there are wrongs that need me for the righting,
While there is warfare splendid and divine.

Give me for light the sunshine of Thy sorrow,
Give me for shelter shadow of Thy Cross,
Give me to share the glory of Thy morrow,
Gone from my heart is the bitterness of loss.

Good-bye, Roy, old chap. I will write to the mother and tell her not to think of you as lying in a grave, but as standing to attention, glad and full of life, before the great White Captain of all souls. Some day we shall meet. Some day she and I will recognise you in a new and glorious body, quite different from this poor broken flesh, and yet in difference still the same, because there will be shining in it and through it the gallant, splendid spirit that is Roy, best of soldiers, best of servants, best of pals.

Postscript

A REPLY TO SOME CRITICISM AND A FEW WORDS TO ANY READERS WHO MAY BE HURT BY WHAT I HAVE WRITTEN

SOME very wise and good people have been hurt by what I have written when they read it in printers proof. There may be many like them. As my object is to help and not to hurt, I would humbly beg my readers to take into account some of the following considerations before they pass final judgment on a very poor attempt to express the inexpressible.

This is not a theological essay. I doubt if I could write one, and I am sure that no one would read it if I did. This is a fairly faithful and accurate account of the inner ruminations of an incurably religious man under battle conditions. I think this accounts for many things. It accounts for what my critics have called a " lack of balance " which runs through it, the predominance of the one idea. Battles do not make for carefully balanced thought. There is one main idea in what I have written, but I believe that it is a true idea. We must make clear to ourselves and to the world what we mean when we say " I believe in God the Father Almighty." The conditions under which these meditations were made account for the repeated and constant denial of the popular conception. I may have railed at that conception very fiercely, but my raillery is mild and good-natured compared with the outspoken comments of the guns. This also accounts for the style. Good people have told me that it is crude and brutal. I would remind you that it is not, and it could not be as crude as war, or as brutal as a battle. I have not really violated what John Oxenham has finely called " the most loving conspiracy of silence the world has ever known," or torn aside the veil of noble reticence behind which our soldiers seek to hide the sufferings they endure. I would not if I could, and I could not if I would. I would not if I could, because it would be cruel. I

could not if I would, because the brutality of war is literally unutterable. There are no words foul and filthy enough to describe it. Yet I would remind you that this indescribably filthy thing is the commonest thing in History, and that if we believe in a God of Love at all we must believe in the face of war and all it means. The supreme strength of the Christian faith is that it faces the foulest and filthiest of life s facts in the crude brutality of the Cross, and through them sees the Glory of God in the
face of Jesus Christ. Thousands of men who have fought out here, and thousands of their womenkind who have waited or mourned for them at home, have dimly felt that the reason and explanation of all this horror was somehow to be found in a Crucifix witness the frequent reproductions of wayside Calvaries in our picture papers and the continual mention of them in our soldiers letters home. Yet when you talk to soldiers you find that the Calvary appeals to them rather as the summary of their problems than their solution. They feel that it is like life, but has no light to shed upon life s mysteries. It is to them a thing of the past, a tale of long ago, and except that it seems natural to them now, as it stands in the midst of a battered village among broken, tired men, it has no relation to their present problems or their present needs. Their only comment, seldom spoken, but often thought, is, " He died to save us from our sin, and there is this, only this, after so many years." But all the pondering about life which has been done out here has been slowly bearing fruit, and a fresh light is beginning to glimmer through the darkness. Men are beginning to see a fresh vision of God in Christ. If I believed that the point of view expressed in this book was peculiarly my own, and was in that sense original, I would not have bothered to write it down. But I don t, I believe it is in the minds of thousands who have neither time nor words to express it. It is in the air. It is the vision of God that war has shown to many. This fact does not guarantee its truth, but gives to it a value.

But that is just the weakness of it, some of my critics have said. It is a partial theology, a distorted truth which appeals to men in the awful conditions of War, but the return of Peace 1 and Peace conditions will make it seem lopsided and absurd. I do not think so, unless Peace brings in the Millennium, and though I am an optimist I do not anticipate that. The Vision of the Suffering God revealed in Jesus Christ, and the necessary Truth of it, first began to dawn on me in the narrow streets and shadowed homes of an English slum. All that War has done is to batter the essential Truth of it deeper in, and cast a fiercer light upon the Cross. A battle field is more striking, but scarcely more really crude and brutal than a slum. Only we have all been suddenly forced to realise war more or less, while it has taken God centuries to make some of us recognise the existence of slums. Soldiers are not the only people who have their conspiracy of silence. Scientists, doctors, travellers, and social workers have their conspiracies too, which decency forces them to observe. Yet facts are none the less facts because they are beastly, and though we may not talk about -them we must take them into account. The more deeply you delve into the facts of life the more utterly incredible the idea of absolute unlimited Omnipotence becomes. The burden of crude brutality which is laid upon God in this book is as nothing to the awful burden God has to bear.

My critics have some of them said that the Church as a whole has never taught this doctrine of Omnipotence absolute and unlimited. It is difficult to discover any thing beyond the simple Christian facts which the Church as a whole has always taught her children. The facts remain constant, the interpretation of them changes. This much, however, is certain that, whether the Church has taught it or not, thousands of her children have learnt the conception of God as One who can do any thing He likes whenever He likes, and the effort to square that conception with facts is wrecking their faith.

It is true that the doctrine of free-will has been constantly preached, and men taught to recognise that this limited the power of God for good. But this great Truth has been taught as a " self- limitation" of God, as if God could have made men perfect without it, but chose to give it them, thus casting back upon God the moral burden of its misuse. Moreover, it has been taught as if it accounted for all the evil in the world, and it doesn't. It fails to touch the misery that is caused not by knaves but by honest fools, and that is great. It fails to account for the changing standards of right and wrong in different ages, and different countries. It has nothing to say to the cruelties of nature, to disease, insanity, idiocy, which are hidden by the world s great conspiracy of silence about unpleasant things. It has to be modified to allow for the enormous and inevitable influence of heredity and environment upon the will, and so upon conscience and character. To say that a man born in a slum or in Berlin is entirely responsible for his actions is to go beyond the obvious truth, while to say that he is not responsible at all is to fall disastrously short of it.

This sketch of a book is palpably inadequate. It just takes a truth and hurls it at your head as the guns hurled it at mine, only it is comparatively gentle hurling. But a greater " Hardest Part " could be written by a worthier brain and hand which could make the Truth inevitably clear and cogent. All the more clear and all the more cogent when placed in its proper relation to the rest of Truth, and not isolated as it stands here.

One great objection remains. Does not the solution of the whole problem lie in the mystery of time ? We are creatures of time and God is eternal and beyond time, we cannot hope to understand His ways or judge them by our puny human standards. This sounds the wise, large-minded, and reverent thing to say. But alas ! it goes too far, and proves too much. If I cannot judge God s ways by human standards, that is by the standard set by Christ for men, then I cannot judge my own ways by God's standards, since I am, and must be, ignorant of what they are. If that is true there is an end to ethical religion. If the eternal standards of Right and Wrong differ from the temporal standards revealed to us by Christ, then I am making an empty statement when I say that God is good. If that statement is empty, then life is empty and I have no religion, for I cannot worship any God who is not good in the Christian sense. Therein lies the point and poignancy of the whole problem. It is not an intellectual but a moral problem. The popular conception of omnipotence sets up an opposition between our religion and our highest moral values, an opposition which is disastrous to both. This worship of a God so great that He is above Right and Wrong has already led to two terrible but common results. It has led to the easy tolerance by Christian people of social wrongs which are a burning disgrace because they sacrificed their moral standards to their religion, and it has led to the abandonment of religion by many noble souls who sacrificed their religion to their moral standards.

It amounts to this. Religion is impossible when we try to do without or go beyond the Incarnation. Metaphysical speculation which tries to go beyond the God in man and find the God Absolute is valueless from a living and religious point of view. The Rock of Ages is the Divinity of Christ, and in Him there lies the solution of our problems, and the inspiration of our lives. He can bear all the weight we can throw upon Him, and does bear it, for He is God. I go back to the Cross with the Empty Tomb behind it, and there I find a satisfying and inspiring answer to it all.

> Thou who dost dwell in depths of timeless being,
> Watching the years as moments passing by.
> Seeing the things that lie beyond our seeing,
> Constant, unchanged as aeons dawn and die;
>
> Thou who canst count the stars upon their courses,

The Hardest Part

Holding them all in the hollow of Thy hand,
Lord of the world with all its million forces,
Seeing the hills as single grains of sand;

Art Thou so great that all our bitter crying,
Sounds in Thine ears as sorrow of a child ?
Hast Thou looked down on centuries of sighing,
And, like a heartless mother, only smiled ?

Since in Thy sight to-day is as to-morrow,
And while we strive Thy victory is won,
Hast Thou no tears to shed upon our sorrow ?
Art Thou a staring splendour like the sun ?

Dost Thou not heed the helpless sparrow s falling ?
Dost Thou not mourn the lost and wandering sheep ?
Canst Thou not hear Thy littlest children calling ?
Dost Thou not watch above them as they sleep ?

Then, O my God, Thou art too great to love me,
Since Thou dost reign beyond the reach of tears,
Calm and serene as the cruel stars abore me,
High and remote from human hopes and fears.

Only in Him can I find Home to hide me,
Who on the Cross was slain to rise again,
Only with Him my comrade God beside me,
Can I go forth to war with sin and pain.

There is the real God. In Him I find no metaphysical abstraction, but God speaking to me in the only language I can understand, which is the human language, God revealed in the only terms I can begin to comprehend, which are the terms of perfect Human Personality. In Him I find the Truth that human sin and sorrow matter to God, nay, are matters of life and death to God, as they must be to me. In Him I find the Truth that the moral struggle of man is a real struggle because God is in it, in it and beyond it too, for in the Risen Christ who conquered death and rose again I find the promise and the guarantee that the moral struggle of the race will issue in victory. In Him I still can stand and say my Creed from the bottom of my heart. For there is a sense in which I believe more firmly than I ever did before that God is Almighty. I can still stand facing East whence comes the Dawn, and say " I believe in God the Father Almighty," and in those glorious words confess my faith that the final Victory of God is as sure, nay, surer than the rising of to-morrow s sun. God is suffering His agony now, but the day will surely come when His agony and ours will be ended, and we shall sing our song of praise to the triumphant God of Love (cp. pp. 91, 92). Sin and sorrow, though real, are only temporary, the results of temporary and contingent necessities inherent in the task of creation, but they will pass away, and God will prove Himself Almighty in the end.

I have shouted out the negative " Not Almighty " again and again against the popular conception because life in Peace and War shouts it out at me. But the negative is only important so far as it clears away the clouds that hide the great Positive of the All-conquering God revealed in Christ.

In conclusion, my friends have been grieved because I made jokes about serious subjects and serious people. In such matters one should be " dead serious " I have been told. That is a point of view which it is difficult for an Irishman to understand at any time, but is doubly difficult for one who has served with the armies at the front. Out here making fun is the most serious business of our lives. I doubt if it is possible, and I am sure it is not wholesome for any living man to be " dead serious." To lack a sense of humour is one of the most terrible handicaps in life for anyone, and is a disaster in a writer or a preacher who wants to help. I have often suspected that what Mr. H. G. Wells really lacks is a genuine loving sense of humour. He thought he had dismissed Bishops when he said they were " jokes." But if a Bishop is a good joke, he may be still one of the best and lightest things in the world. I have made fun of the Arch bishop of Canterbury, but I firmly believe that he is one of the Tightest and best people in England. Christian laughter always hovers just on the brink of tears, for God in Christ has redeemed them both and wedded joy to sorrow, and real peace to pain.

If anything I have said sounds like contempt or disrespect to the English Church or her teachers, it is not so meant. Honest criticism and difference of opinion is not disrespect, and that is all I have meant to express.

It is all very poor and incomplete. But better and wiser men than I will put that right by picking it to pieces, if they think it worth their while. So Truth grows stronger, and that is all that matters.

I wish I could write it over again, but it would be worse next time. Anyhow, kind reader, think again before you cast it out.

G. A. STUDDERT KENNEDY,

Army Infantry School,
B.E.F.

Printed in Great Britain
by Amazon